The Complete Works Of Henry Wadsworth Longfellow

Mary E. Bush
Fall River
Aug 7th 1872   Mass

THE

COMPLETE WORKS

OF

HENRY WADSWORTH LONGFELLOW

REVISED EDITION

VOL. II.

THE BELFRY OF BRUGES AND OTHER POEMS. — EVAN-
GELINE. — THE SEASIDE AND THE FIRESIDE.

BOSTON:
JAMES R. OSGOOD AND COMPANY,
LATE TICKNOR & FIELDS, AND FIELDS, OSGOOD, & CO.
1872.

Entered according to Act of Congress, in the year 1866, by
HENRY WADSWORTH LONGFELLOW,
in the Clerk's Office of the District Court of the District of Massachusetts.

UNIVERSITY PRESS: WELCH, BIGELOW, & CO.,
CAMBRIDGE.

CONTENTS

Contents

THE BELFRY OF BRUGES

AND OTHER POEMS

1845

CARILLON

IN the ancient town of Bruges,
 In the quaint old Flemish city,
As the evening shades descended,
Low and loud and sweetly blended,
Low at times and loud at times,
And changing like a poet's rhymes,
Rang the beautiful wild chimes
From the Belfry in the market
Of the ancient town of Bruges.

Then, with deep sonorous clangor
Calmly answering their sweet anger,
When the wrangling bells had ended,
Slowly struck the clock eleven,
And, from out the silent heaven,
Silence on the town descended.
Silence, silence everywhere,
On the earth and in the air,
Save that footsteps here and there
Of some burgher home returning,
By the street lamps faintly burning,

For a moment woke the echoes
Of the ancient town of Bruges.

But amid my broken slumbers
Still I heard those magic numbers,
As they loud proclaimed the flight
And stolen marches of the night;
Till their chimes in sweet collision
Mingled with each wandering vision,
Mingled with the fortune-telling
Gypsy-bands of dreams and fancies,
Which amid the waste expanses
Of the silent land of trances
Have their solitary dwelling;
All else seemed asleep in Bruges,
In the quaint old Flemish city.

And I thought how like these chimes
Are the poet's airy rhymes,
All his rhymes and roundelays,
His conceits, and songs, and ditties,
From the belfry of his brain,
Scattered downward, though in vain,
On the roofs and stones of cities!
For by night the drowsy ear
Under its curtains cannot hear,
And by day men go their ways,
Hearing the music as they pass,

But deeming it no more, alas!
Than the hollow sound of brass.

Yet perchance a sleepless wight,
Lodging at some humble inn
In the narrow lanes of life,
When the dusk and hush of night
Shut out the incessant din
Of daylight and its toil and strife,
May listen with a calm delight
To the poet's melodies,
Till he hears, or dreams he hears,
Intermingled with the song,
Thoughts that he has cherished long;
·Hears amid the chime and singing
The bells of his own village ringing,
And wakes, and finds his slumberous eyes
Wet with most delicious tears.

Thus dreamed I, as by night I lay
In Bruges, at the Fleur-de-Blé,
Listening with a wild delight
To the chimes that, through the night,
Rang their changes from the Belfry
Of that quaint old Flemish city.

THE BELFRY OF BRUGES

IN the market-place of Bruges stands the belfry .
    old and brown ;
Thrice consumed and thrice rebuilded, still it
    watches o'er the town.

As the summer morn was breaking, on that lofty
    tower I stood,
And the world threw off the darkness, like the
    weeds of widowhood.

Thick with towns and hamlets studded, and with
    streams and vapors gray,
Like a shield embossed with silver, round and vast
    the landscape lay.

At my feet the city slumbered. From its chim-
    neys, here and there,
Wreaths of snow-white smoke, ascending, vanished,
    ghost-like, into air.

Not a sound rose from the city at that early morn-
    ing hour,
But I heard a heart of iron beating in the ancient
    tower.

From their nests beneath the rafters sang the
    swallows wild and high ;
And the world, beneath me sleeping, seemed more
    distant than the sky.

Then most musical and solemn, bringing back the
    olden times,
With their strange, unearthly changes rang the
    melancholy chimes,

Like the psalms from some old cloister, when the
    nuns sing in the choir ;
And the great bell tolled among them, like the
    chanting of a friar.

Visions of the days departed, shadowy phantoms
    filled my brain ;
They who live in history only seemed to walk the
    earth again ;

All the Foresters of Flanders, — mighty Baldwin
    Bras de Fer,
Lyderick du Bucq and Cressy, Philip, Guy de
    Dampierre.

I beheld the pageants splendid that adorned those
  days of old ;
Stately dames, like queens attended, knights who
  bore the Fleece of Gold

Lombard and Venetian merchants with deep-laden
  argosies ;
Ministers from twenty nations ; more than royal
  pomp and ease.

I beheld proud Maximilian, kneeling humbly on
  the ground ;
I beheld the gentle Mary, hunting with her hawk
  and hound ;

And her lighted bridal-chamber, where a duke
  slept with the queen,
And the armed guard around them, and the sword
  unsheathed between.

I beheld the Flemish weavers, with Namur and
  Juliers bold,
Marching homeward from the bloody battle of the
  Spurs of Gold ;

Saw the fight at Minnewater, saw the White
  Hoods moving west,
Saw great Artevelde victorious scale the Golden
  Dragon's nest.

  I *

And again the whiskered Spaniard all the land
      with terror smote ;
And again the wild alarum sounded from the
      tocsin's throat ;

Till the bell of Ghent responded o'er lagoon and
      dike of sand,
"I am Roland ! I am Roland ! there is victory in
      the land ! "

Then the sound of drums aroused me.   The awak-
      ened city's roar
Chased the phantoms I had summoned back into
      their graves once more.

Hours had passed away like minutes ; and, before
      I was aware,
Lo ! the shadow of the belfry crossed the sun-illu-
      mined square.

MISCELLANEOUS

A GLEAM OF SUNSHINE

THIS is the place.   Stand still, my steed,
  Let me review the scene,
And summon from the shadowy Past
  The forms that once have been.

The Past and Present here unite
  Beneath Time's flowing tide,
Like footprints hidden by a brook,
  But seen on either side.

Here runs the highway to the town ;
  There the green lane descends,
Through which I walked to church with thee,
  O gentlest of my friends !

The shadow of the linden-trees
  Lay moving on the grass ;
Between them and the moving boughs,
  A shadow, thou didst pass.

Thy dress was like the lilies,
    And thy heart as pure as they:
One of God's holy messengers
    Did walk with me that day.

I saw the branches of the trees
    Bend down thy touch to meet,
The clover-blossoms in the grass
    Rise up to kiss thy feet.

" Sleep, sleep to-day, tormenting cares,
    Of earth and folly born ! "
Solemnly sang the village choir
    On that sweet Sabbath morn.

Through the closed blinds the golden sun
    Poured in a dusty beam,
Like the celestial ladder seen
    By Jacob in his dream.

And ever and anon, the wind,
    Sweet-scented with the hay,
Turned o'er the hymn-book's fluttering leaves
    That on the window lay.

Long was the good man's sermon,
    Yet it seemed not so to me ;
For he spake of Ruth the beautiful,
    And still I thought of thee.

Long was the prayer he uttered,
  Yet it seemed not so to me;
For in my heart I prayed with him,
  And still I thought of thee.

But now, alas! the place seems changed;
  Thou art no longer here:
Part of the sunshine of the scene
  With thee did disappear.

Though thoughts, deep-rooted in my heart,
  Like pine-trees dark and high,
Subdue the light of noon, and breathe
  A low and ceaseless sigh;

This memory brightens o'er the past,
  As when the sun, concealed
Behind some cloud that near us hangs,
  Shines on a distant field.

THE ARSENAL AT SPRINGFIELD

THIS is the Arsenal.   From floor to ceiling,
  Like a huge organ, rise the burnished arms;
But from their silent pipes no anthem pealing
  Startles the villages with strange alarms.

Ah ! what a sound will rise, how wild and dreary,
  When the death-angel touches those swift keys !
What loud lament and dismal Miserere
  Will mingle with their awful symphonies !

I hear even now the infinite fierce chorus,
  The cries of agony, the endless groan,
Which, through the ages that have gone before us,
  In long reverberations reach our own.

On helm and harness rings the Saxon hammer,
  Through Cimbric forest roars the Norseman's
                song,
And loud, amid the universal clamor,
  O'er distant deserts sounds the Tartar gong.

I hear the Florentine, who from his palace
  Wheels out his battle-bell with dreadful din,
And Aztec priests upon their teocallis
  Beat the wild war-drums made of serpent's skin ;

The tumult of each sacked and burning village ;
  The shout that every prayer for mercy drowns ;
The soldiers' revels in the midst of pillage ;
  The wail of famine in beleaguered towns ;

The bursting shell, the gateway wrenched asunder,
  The rattling musketry, the clashing blade ;
And ever and anon, in tones of thunder,
  The diapason of the cannonade.

Is it, O man, with such discordant noises,
    With such accursed instruments as these,
Thou drownest Nature's sweet and kindly voices,
    And jarrest the celestial harmonies?

Were half the power, that fills the world with terror,
    Were half the wealth, bestowed on camps and
        courts,
Given to redeem the human mind from error,
    There were no need of arsenals or forts :

The warrior's name would be a name abhorred !
    And every nation, that should lift again
Its hand against a brother, on its forehead
    Would wear forevermore the curse of Cain !

Down the dark future, through long generations,
    The echoing sounds grow fainter and then cease ;
And like a bell, with solemn, sweet vibrations,
    I hear once more the voice of Christ say,
        " Peace ! "

Peace ! and no longer from its brazen portals
    The blast of War's great organ shakes the
        skies !
But beautiful as songs of the immortals,
    The holy melodies of love arise.

NUREMBERG

IN the valley of the Pegnitz, where across broad
    meadow-lands
Rise the blue Franconian mountains, Nuremberg,
    the ancient, stands.

Quaint old town of toil and traffic, quaint old town
    of art and song,
Memories haunt thy pointed gables, like the rooks
    that round them throng:

Memories of the Middle Ages, when the emperors,
    rough and bold,
Had their dwelling in thy castle, time-defying,
    centuries old;

And thy brave and thrifty burghers boasted, in
    their uncouth rhyme,
That their great imperial city stretched its hand
    through every clime.

In the court-yard of the castle, bound with many
    an iron band,
Stands the mighty linden planted by Queen Cuni-
    gunde's hand;

On the square the oriel window, where in old
    heroic days
Sat the poet Melchior singing Kaiser Maximilian's
    praise.

Everywhere I see around me rise the wondrous
    world of Art:
Fountains wrought with richest sculpture standing
    in the common mart;

And above cathedral doorways saints and bishops
    carved in stone,
By a former age commissioned as apostles to our
    own.

In the church of sainted Sebald sleeps enshrined
    his holy dust,
And in bronze the Twelve Apostles guard from
    age to age their trust;

In the church of sainted Lawrence stands a pix of
    sculpture rare,
Like the foamy sheaf of fountains, rising through
    the painted air.

Here, when Art was still religion, with a simple,
    reverent heart,
Lived and labored Albrecht Dürer, the Evangelist
    of Art;

Hence in silence and in sorrow, toiling still with
    busy hand,
Like an emigrant he wandered, seeking for the
    Better Land.

Emigravit is the inscription on the tombstone
    where he lies ;
Dead he is not, but departed, — for the artist never
    dies.

Fairer seems the ancient city, and the sunshine
    seems more fair,
That he once has trod its pavement, that he once
    has breathed its air !

Through these streets so broad and stately, these
    obscure and dismal lanes,
Walked of yore the Mastersingers, chanting rude
    poetic strains.

From remote and sunless suburbs came they to
    the friendly guild,
Building nests in Fame's great temple, as in spouts
    the swallows build.

As the weaver plied the shuttle, wove he too the
    mystic rhyme,
And the smith his iron measures hammered to the
    anvil's chime ;

Thanking God, whose boundless wisdom makes
    the flowers of poesy bloom
In the forge's dust and cinders, in the tissues of
    the loom.

Here Hans Sachs, the cobbler-poet, laureate of the
    gentle craft,
Wisest of the Twelve Wise Masters, in huge folios
    sang and laughed.

But his house is now an ale-house, with a nicely
    sanded floor,
And a garland in the window, and his face above
    the door;

Painted by some humble artist, as in Adam Pusch-
    man's song,
As the old man gray and dove-like, with his great
    beard white and long.

And at night the swart mechanic comes to drown
    his cark and care,
Quaffing ale from pewter tankards, in the master's
    antique chair.

Vanished is the ancient splendor, and before my
    dreamy eye
Wave these mingling shapes and figures, like a
    faded tapestry.

Not thy Councils, not thy Kaisers, win for thee the
    world's regard ;
But thy painter, Albrecht Dürer, and Hans Sachs
    thy cobbler-bard.

Thus, O Nuremberg, a wanderer from a region far
    away,
As he paced thy streets and court-yards, sang in
    thought his careless lay :

Gathering from the pavement's crevice, as a flow-
    eret of the soil,
The nobility of labor, — the long pedigree of
    toil.

THE NORMAN BARON

Dans les moments de la vie où la réflexion devient plus calme et plus
profonde, où l'intérêt et l'avarice parlent moins haut que la raison, dans
les instants de chagrin domestique, de maladie, et de péril de mort, les
nobles se repentirent de posséder des serfs, comme d'une chose peu agré-
able à Dieu, qui avait créé tous les hommes à son image.

                THIERRY : CONQUÊTE DE L'ANGLETERRE.

I N his chamber, weak and dying,
    Was the Norman baron lying ;
Loud, without, the tempest thundered,
    And the castle-turret shook.

In this fight was Death the gainer,
Spite of vassal and retainer,
And the lands his sires had plundered,
    Written in the Doomsday Book.

By his bed a monk was seated,
Who in humble voice repeated
Many a prayer and pater-noster,
    From the missal on his knee;

And, amid the tempest pealing,
Sounds of bells came faintly stealing,
Bells, that from the neighboring kloster
    Rang for the Nativity.

In the hall, the serf and vassal
Held, that night, their Christmas wassail;
Many a carol, old and saintly,
    Sang the minstrels and the waits;

And so loud these Saxon gleemen
Sang to slaves the songs of freemen,
That the storm was heard but faintly,
    Knocking at the castle-gates.

Till at length the lays they chanted
Reached the chamber terror-haunted,
Where the monk, with accents holy,
    Whispered at the baron's ear.

Tears upon his eyelids glistened,
As he paused awhile and listened,
And the dying baron slowly
    Turned his weary head to hear.

"Wassail for the kingly stranger
Born and cradled in a manger!
King, like David, priest, like Aaron,
    Christ is born to set us free!"

And the lightning showed the sainted
Figures on the casement painted,
And exclaimed the shuddering baron,
    "Miserere, Domine!"

In that hour of deep contrition
He beheld, with clearer vision,
Through all outward show and fashion,
    Justice, the Avenger, rise.

All the pomp of earth had vanished,
Falsehood and deceit were banished,
Reason spake more loud than passion,
    And the truth wore no disguise.

Every vassal of his banner,
Every serf born to his manor,
All those wronged and wretched creatures,
    By his hand were freed again.

And, as on the sacred missal
He recorded their dismissal,
Death relaxed his iron features,
 And the monk replied, " Amen ! "

Many centuries have been numbered
Since in death the baron slumbered
By the convent's sculptured portal,
 Mingling with the common dust :

But the good deed, through the ages
Living in historic pages,
Brighter grows and gleams immortal,
 Unconsumed by moth or rust.

RAIN IN SUMMER

HOW beautiful is the rain !
 After the dust and heat,
In the broad and fiery street,
In the narrow lane,
How beautiful is the rain !

How it clatters along the roofs,
Like the tramp of hoofs !
How it gushes and struggles out
From the throat of the overflowing spout !

Across the window pane
It pours and pours ;
And swift and wide,
With a muddy tide,
Like a river down the gutter roars
The rain, the welcome rain !

The sick man from his chamber looks
At the twisted brooks ;
He can feel the cool
Breath of each little pool ;
His fevered brain
Grows calm again,
And he breathes a blessing on the rain.

From the neighboring school
Come the boys,
With more than their wonted noise
And commotion ;
And down the wet streets
Sail their mimic fleets,
Till the treacherous pool
Engulfs them in its whirling
And turbulent ocean.

In the country, on every side,
Where far and wide,
Like a leopard's tawny and spotted hide,
Stretches the plain,

To the dry grass and the drier grain
How welcome is the rain !

In the furrowed land
The toilsome and patient oxen stand ;
Lifting the yoke-encumbered head,
With their dilated nostrils spread,
They silently inhale
The clover-scented gale,
And the vapors that arise
From the well watered and smoking soil.
For this rest in the furrow after toil
Their large and lustrous eyes
Seem to thank the Lord,
More than man's spoken word.

Near at hand,
From under the sheltering trees,
The farmer sees
His pastures, and his fields of grain,
As they bend their tops
To the numberless beating drops
Of the incessant rain.
He counts it as no sin
That he sees therein
Only his own thrift and gain.

These, and far more than these,
The Poet sees !

He can behold
Aquarius old
Walking the fenceless fields of air;
And from each ample fold
Of the clouds about him rolled
Scattering everywhere
The showery rain,
As the farmer scatters his grain.

He can behold
Things manifold
That have not yet been wholly told, —
Have not been wholly sung nor said.
For his thought, that never stops,
Follows the water-drops
Down to the graves of the dead,
Down through chasms and gulfs profound,
To the dreary fountain-head
Of lakes and rivers under ground;
And sees them, when the rain is done,
On the bridge of colors seven
Climbing up once more to heaven,
Opposite the setting sun.

Thus the Seer,
With vision clear,
Sees forms appear and disappear,
In the perpetual round of strange,
Mysterious change

From birth to death, from death to birth,
From earth to heaven, from heaven to earth;
Till glimpses more sublime
Of things, unseen before,
Unto his wondering eyes reveal
The Universe, as an immeasurable wheel
Turning forevermore
In the rapid and rushing river of Time.

TO A CHILD

DEAR child! how radiant on thy mother's knee,
   With merry-making eyes and jocund smiles,
Thou gazest at the painted tiles,
Whose figures grace,
With many a grotesque form and face,
The ancient chimney of thy nursery!
The lady with the gay macaw,
The dancing girl, the grave bashaw
With bearded lip and chin;
And, leaning idly o'er his gate,
Beneath the imperial fan of state,
The Chinese mandarin.

With what a look of proud command
Thou shakest in thy little hand

The coral rattle with its silver bells,
Making a merry tune!
Thousands of years in Indian seas
That coral grew, by slow degrees,
Until some deadly and wild monsoon
Dashed it on Coromandel's sand!
Those silver bells
Reposed of yore,
As shapeless ore,
Far down in the deep-sunken wells
Of darksome mines,
In some obscure and sunless place,
Beneath huge Chimborazo's base,
Or Potosí's o'erhanging pines!
And thus for thee, O little child,
Through many a danger and escape,
The tall ships passed the stormy cape;
For thee in foreign lands remote,
Beneath a burning, tropic clime,
The Indian peasant, chasing the wild goat,
Himself as swift and wild,
In falling, clutched the frail arbute,
The fibres of whose shallow root,
Uplifted from the soil, betrayed
The silver veins beneath it laid,
The buried treasures of the miser, Time.

But, lo! thy door is left ajar!
Thou hearest footsteps from afar!

And, at the sound,
Thou turnest round
With quick and questioning eyes,
Like one, who, in a foreign land,
Beholds on every hand
Some source of wonder and surprise!
And, restlessly, impatiently,
Thou strivest, strugglest, to be free.
The four walls of thy nursery
Are now like prison walls to thee.
No more thy mother's smiles,
No more the painted tiles,
Delight thee, nor the playthings on the floor,
That won thy little, beating heart before;
Thou strugglest for the open door.

Through these once solitary halls
Thy pattering footstep falls.
The sound of thy merry voice
Makes the old walls
Jubilant, and they rejoice
With the joy of thy young heart,
O'er the light of whose gladness
No shadows of sadness
From the sombre background of memory start.

Once, ah, once, within these walls,
One whom memory oft recalls,
The Father of his Country, dwelt.

And yonder meadows broad and damp
The fires of the besieging camp
Encircled with a burning belt.
Up and down these echoing stairs,
Heavy with the weight of cares,
Sounded his majestic tread ;
Yes, within this very room
Sat he in those hours of gloom,
Weary both in heart and head.

But what are these grave thoughts to thee ?
Out, out ! into the open air !
Thy only dream is liberty,
Thou carest little how or where.
I see thee eager at thy play,
Now shouting to the apples on the tree,
With cheeks as round and red as they ;
And now among the yellow stalks,
Among the flowering shrubs and plants,
As restless as the bee.
Along the garden walks,
The tracks of thy small carriage-wheels I trace ;
And see at every turn how they efface
Whole villages of sand-roofed tents,
That rise like golden domes
Above the cavernous and secret homes
Of wandering and nomadic tribes of ants.
Ah, cruel little Tamerlane,
Who, with thy dreadful reign,

Dost persecute and overwhelm
These hapless Troglodytes of thy realm!

What! tired already! with those suppliant looks,
And voice more beautiful than a poet's books,
Or murmuring sound of water as it flows,
Thou comest back to parley with repose!
This rustic seat in the old apple-tree,
With its o'erhanging golden canopy
Of leaves illuminate with autumnal hues,
And shining with the argent light of dews,
Shall for a season be our place of rest.
Beneath us, like an oriole's pendent nest,
From which the laughing birds have taken wing,
By thee abandoned, hangs thy vacant swing.
Dream-like the waters of the river gleam;
A sailless vessel drops adown the stream,
And like it, to a sea as wide and deep,
Thou driftest gently down the tides of sleep.

O child! O new-born denizen
Of life's great city! on thy head
The glory of the morn is shed,
Like a celestial benison!
Here at the portal thou dost stand,
And with thy little hand
Thou openest the mysterious gate
Into the future's undiscovered land.
I see its valves expand,

As at the touch of Fate!
Into those realms of love and hate,
Into that darkness blank and drear,
By some prophetic feeling taught,
I launch the bold, adventurous thought,
Freighted with hope and fear;
As upon subterranean streams,
In caverns unexplored and dark,
Men sometimes launch a fragile bark,
Laden with flickering fire,
And watch its swift-receding beams,
Until at length they disappear,
And in the distant dark expire.

By what astrology of fear or hope
Dare I to cast thy horoscope!
Like the new moon thy life appears;
A little strip of silver light,
And widening outward into night
The shadowy disk of future years;
And yet upon its outer rim,
A luminous circle, faint and dim,
And scarcely visible to us here,
Rounds and completes the perfect sphere;
A prophecy and intimation,
A pale and feeble adumbration,
Of the great world of light, that lies
Behind all human destinies.

Ah! if thy fate, with anguish fraught,
· Should be to wet the dusty soil
With the hot tears and sweat of toil, —
To struggle with imperious thought,
Until the overburdened brain,
Weary with labor, faint with pain,
Like a jarred pendulum, retain
Only its motion, not its power, —
Remember, in that perilous hour,
When most afflicted and oppressed,
From labor there shall come forth rest.

And if a more auspicious fate
On thy advancing steps await,
Still let it ever be thy pride
To linger by the laborer's side ;
With words of sympathy or song
To cheer the dreary march along
Of the great army of the poor,
O'er desert sand, o'er dangerous moor.
Nor to thyself the task shall be
Without reward ; for thou shalt learn
The wisdom early to discern
True beauty in utility ;
As great Pythagoras of yore,
Standing beside the blacksmith's door,
And hearing the hammers, as they smote
The anvils with a different note,
Stole from the varying tones, that hung

Vibrant on every iron tongue,
The secret of the sounding wire,
And formed the seven-chorded lyre.

Enough ! I will not play the Seer ;
I will no longer strive to ope
The mystic volume, where appear
The herald Hope, forerunning Fear,
And Fear, the pursuivant of Hope.
Thy destiny remains untold ;
For, like Acestes' shaft of old,
The swift thought kindles as it flies,
And burns to ashes in the skies.

THE OCCULTATION OF ORION

I SAW, as in a dream sublime,
   The balance in the hand of Time.
O'er East and West its beam impended ;
And day, with all its hours of light,
Was slowly sinking out of sight,
While, opposite, the scale of night
Silently with the stars ascended.

Like the astrologers of eld,
In that bright vision I beheld

Greater and deeper mysteries.
I saw, with its celestial keys,
Its chords of air, its frets of fire,
The Samian's great Æolian lyre,
Rising through all its sevenfold bars,
From earth unto the fixed stars.
And through the dewy atmosphere,
Not only could I see, but hear,
Its wondrous and harmonious strings,
In sweet vibration, sphere by sphere,
From Dian's circle light and near,
Onward to vaster and wider rings,
Where, chanting through his beard of snows,
Majestic, mournful, Saturn goes,
And down the sunless realms of space
Reverberates the thunder of his bass.

Beneath the sky's triumphal arch
This music sounded like a march,
And with its chorus seemed to be
Preluding some great tragedy.
Sirius was rising in the east ;
And, slow ascending one by one,
The kindling constellations shone.
Begirt with many a blazing star,
Stood the great giant Algebar,
Orion, hunter of the beast !
His sword hung gleaming by his side,
And, on his arm, the lion's hide

Scattered across the midnight air
The golden radiance of its hair.

The moon was pallid, but not faint;
And beautiful as some fair saint,
Serenely moving on her way
In hours of trial and dismay.
As if she heard the voice of God,
Unharmed with naked feet she trod
Upon the hot and burning stars,
As on the glowing coals and bars,
That were to prove her strength, and try
Her holiness and her purity.

Thus moving on, with silent pace,
And triumph in her sweet, pale face,
She reached the station of Orion.
Aghast he stood in strange alarm!
And suddenly from his outstretched arm
Down fell the red skin of the lion
Into the river at his feet.
His mighty club no longer beat
The forehead of the bull; but he
Reeled as of yore beside the sea,
When, blinded by Œnopion,
He sought the blacksmith at his forge,
And, climbing up the mountain gorge,
Fixed his blank eyes upon the sun.

Then, through the silence overhead,
An angel with a trumpet said,
"Forevermore, forevermore,
The reign of violence is o'er!"
And, like an instrument that flings
Its music on another's strings,
The trumpet of the angel cast
Upon the heavenly lyre its blast,
And on from sphere to sphere the words
Re-echoed down the burning chords, —
"Forevermore, forevermore,
The reign of violence is o'er!"

THE BRIDGE

I STOOD on the bridge at midnight,
  As the clocks were striking the hour,
And the moon rose o'er the city,
  Behind the dark church-tower.

I saw her bright reflection
  In the waters under me,
Like a golden goblet falling
  And sinking into the sea.

And far in the hazy distance
  Of that lovely night in June,
The blaze of the flaming furnace
  Gleamed redder than the moon.

Among the long, black rafters
  The wavering shadows lay,
And the current that came from the ocean
  Seemed to lift and bear them away;

As, sweeping and eddying through them,
  Rose the belated tide,
And, streaming into the moonlight,
  The seaweed floated wide.

And like those waters rushing
  Among the wooden piers,
A flood of thoughts came o'er me
  That filled my eyes with tears.

How often, O how often,
  In the days that had gone by,
I had stood on that bridge at midnight
  And gazed on that wave and sky!

How often, O how often,
  I had wished that the ebbing tide
Would bear me away on its bosom
  O'er the ocean wild and wide!

For my heart was hot and restless,
　　And my life was full of care,
And the burden laid upon me
　　Seemed greater than I could bear.

But now it has fallen from me,
　　It is buried in the sea ;
And only the sorrow of others
　　Throws its shadow over me.

Yet whenever I cross the river
　　On its bridge with wooden piers,
Like the odor of brine from the ocean
　　Comes the thought of other years.

And I think how many thousands
　　Of care-encumbered men,
Each bearing his burden of sorrow,
　　Have crossed the bridge since then.

I see the long procession
　　Still passing to and fro,
The young heart hot and restless,
　　And the old subdued and slow !

And forever and forever,
　　As long as the river flows,
As long as the heart has passions,
　　As long as life has woes ;

The moon and its broken reflection
And its shadows shall appear,
As the symbol of love in heaven,
And its wavering image here.

TO THE DRIVING CLOUD

GLOOMY and dark art thou, O chief of the
mighty Omahas;
Gloomy and dark as the driving cloud, whose
name thou hast taken!
Wrapt in thy scarlet blanket, I see thee stalk
through the city's
Narrow and populous streets, as once by the margin of rivers
Stalked those birds unknown, that have left us
only their footprints.
What, in a few short years, will remain of thy race
but the footprints?

How canst thou walk these streets, who hast trod
the green turf of the prairies?
How canst thou breathe this air, who hast breathed
the sweet air of the mountains?
Ah! 'tis in vain that with lordly looks of disdain
thou dost challenge

Looks of disdain in return, and question these walls
    and these pavements,
Claiming the soil for thy hunting-grounds, while
    down-trodden millions
Starve in the garrets of Europe, and cry from its
    caverns that they, too,
Have been created heirs of the earth, and claim its
    division!

Back, then, back to thy woods in the regions west
    of the Wabash!
There as a monarch thou reignest. In autumn the
    leaves of the maple
Pave the floors of thy palace-halls with gold, and
    in summer
Pine-trees waft through its chambers the odorous
    breath of their branches.
There thou art strong and great, a hero, a tamer
    of horses!
There thou chasest the stately stag on the banks
    of the Elkhorn,
Or by the roar of the Running-Water, or where the
    Omaha
Calls thee, and leaps through the wild ravine like
    a brave of the Blackfeet!

Hark! what murmurs arise from the heart of those
    mountainous deserts?
Is it the cry of the Foxes and Crows, or the
    mighty Behemoth,

Who, unharmed, on his tusks once caught the bolts
    of the thunder,
And now lurks in his lair to destroy the race of the
    red man?
Far more fatal to thee and thy race than the Crows
    and the Foxes,
Far more fatal to thee and thy race than the tread
    of Behemoth,
Lo! the big thunder-canoe, that steadily breasts
    the Missouri's
Merciless current! and yonder, afar on the prai-
    ries, the camp-fires
Gleam through the night; and the cloud of dust in
    the gray of the daybreak
Marks not the buffalo's track, nor the Mandan's
    dexterous horse-race;
It is a caravan, whitening the desert where dwell
    the Camanches!
Ha! how the breath of these Saxons and Celts,
    like the blast of the east-wind,
Drifts evermore to the west the scanty smokes of
    thy wigwams!

SONGS

SEAWEED

WHEN descends on the Atlantic
    The gigantic
Storm-wind of the equinox,
Landward in his wrath he scourges
    The toiling surges,
Laden with seaweed from the rocks :

From Bermuda's reefs ; from edges
    Of sunken ledges,
In some far-off, bright Azore ;
From Bahama, and the dashing,
    Silver-flashing
Surges of San Salvador ;

From the tumbling surf, that buries
    The Orkneyan skerries,
Answering the hoarse Hebrides ;
And from wrecks of ships, and drifting
    Spars, uplifting
On the desolate, rainy seas ; —

Ever drifting, drifting, drifting
    On the shifting

Currents of the restless main ;
Till in sheltered coves, and reaches
    Of sandy beaches,
All have found repose again.

So when storms of wild emotion
    Strike the ocean
Of the poet's soul, erelong
From each cave and rocky fastness,
    In its vastness,
Floats some fragment of a song :

From the far-off isles enchanted,
    Heaven has planted
With the golden fruit of Truth ;
From the flashing surf, whose vision
    Gleams Elysian
In the tropic clime of Youth ;

From the strong Will, and the Endeavor
    That forever
Wrestles with the tides of Fate ;
From the wreck of Hopes far-scattered,
    Tempest-shattered,
Floating waste and desolate ; —

Ever drifting, drifting, drifting
    On the shifting

Currents of the restless heart;
Till at length in books recorded,
     They, like hoarded
Household words, no more depart.

THE DAY IS DONE

THE day is done, and the darkness
     Falls from the wings of Night,
As a feather is wafted downward
     From an eagle in his flight.

I see the lights of the village
     Gleam through the rain and the mist,
And a feeling of sadness comes o'er me
     That my soul cannot resist:

A feeling of sadness and longing,
     That is not akin to pain,
And resembles sorrow only
     As the mist resembles the rain.

Come, read to me some poem,
     Some simple and heartfelt lay,
That shall soothe this restless feeling,
     And banish the thoughts of day.

Not from the grand old masters,
   Not from the bards sublime,
Whose distant footsteps echo
   Through the corridors of Time.

For, like strains of martial music,
   Their mighty thoughts suggest
Life's endless toil and endeavor;
   And to-night I long for rest.

Read from some humbler poet,
   Whose songs gushed from his heart,
As showers from the clouds of summer,
   Or tears from the eyelids start;

Who, through long days of labor,
   And nights devoid of ease,
Still heard in his soul the music
   Of wonderful melodies.

Such songs have power to quiet
   The restless pulse of care,
And come like the benediction
   That follows after prayer.

Then read from the treasured volume
   The poem of thy choice,
And lend to the rhyme of the poet
   The beauty of thy voice.

And the night shall be filled with music,
  And the cares, that infest the day,
Shall fold their tents, like the Arabs,
  And as silently steal away.

AFTERNOON IN FEBRUARY

THE day is ending,
    The night is descending;
The marsh is frozen,
    The river dead.

Through clouds like ashes
The red sun flashes
On village windows
    That glimmer red.

The snow recommences;
The buried fences
Mark no longer
    The road o'er the plain;

While through the meadows,
Like fearful shadows,
Slowly passes
    A funeral train.

The bell is pealing,
And every feeling
Within me responds
　　To the dismal knell ;

Shadows are trailing,
My heart is bewailing
And tolling within
　　Like a funeral bell.

TO AN OLD DANISH SONG–BOOK

WELCOME, my old friend,
　　Welcome to a foreign fireside,
While the sullen gales of autumn
Shake the windows.

The ungrateful world
Has, it seems, dealt harshly with thee,
Since, beneath the skies of Denmark,
First I met thee.

There are marks of age,
There are thumb-marks on thy margin,
Made by hands that clasped thee rudely,
At the alehouse.

Soiled and dull thou art ;
Yellow are thy time-worn pages,
As the russet, rain-molested
Leaves of autumn.

Thou art stained with wine
Scattered from hilarious goblets,
As the leaves with the libations
Of Olympus.

Yet dost thou recall
Days departed, half-forgotten,
When in dreamy youth I wandered
By the Baltic, —

When I paused to hear
The old ballad of King Christian
Shouted from suburban taverns
In the twilight.

Thou recallest bards,
Who, in solitary chambers,
And with hearts by passion wasted,
Wrote thy pages.

Thou recallest homes
Where thy songs of love and friendship
Made the gloomy Northern winter
Bright as summer.

Once some ancient Scald,
In his bleak, ancestral Iceland,
Chanted staves of these old ballads
To the Vikings.

Once in Elsinore,
At the court of old King Hamlet,
Yorick and his boon companions
Sang these ditties.

Once Prince Frederick's Guard
Sang them in their smoky barracks ; —
Suddenly the English cannon
Joined the chorus !

Peasants in the field,
Sailors on the roaring ocean,
Students, tradesmen, pale mechanics,
All have sung them.

Thou hast been their friend ;
They, alas ! have left thee friendless !
Yet at least by one warm fireside
Art thou welcome.

And, as swallows build
In these wide, old-fashioned chimneys,
So thy twittering songs shall nestle
In my bosom, —

Quiet, close, and warm,
Sheltered from all molestation,
And recalling by their voices
Youth and travel.

WALTER VON DER VOGELWEID

VOGELWEID the Minnesinger,
  When he left this world of ours,
Laid his body in the cloister,
  Under Würtzburg's minster towers.

And he gave the monks his treasures,
  Gave them all with this behest:
They should feed the birds at noontide
  Daily on his place of rest;

Saying, "From these wandering minstrels
  I have learned the art of song;
Let me now repay the lessons
  They have taught so well and long."

Thus the bard of love departed;
  And, fulfilling his desire,
On his tomb the birds were feasted
  By the children of the choir.

Day by day, o'er tower and turret,
  In foul weather and in fair,
Day by day, in vaster numbers,
  Flocked the poets of the air.

On the tree whose heavy branches
  Overshadowed all the place,
On the pavement, on the tombstone,
  On the poet's sculptured face,

On the cross-bars of each window,
  On the lintel of each door,
They renewed the War of Wartburg,
  Which the bard had fought before.

There they sang their merry carols,
  Sang their lauds on every side ;
And the name their voices uttered
  Was the name of Vogelweid.

Till at length the portly abbot
  Murmured, "Why this waste of food?
Be it changed to loaves henceforward
  For our fasting brotherhood."

Then in vain o'er tower and turret,
  From the walls and woodland nests,
When the minster bells rang noontide,
  Gathered the unwelcome guests.

Then in vain, with cries discordant,
　Clamorous round the Gothic spire,
Screamed the feathered Minnesingers
　For the children of the choir.

Time has long effaced the inscriptions
　On the cloister's funeral stones,
And tradition only tells us
　Where repose the poet's bones.

But around the vast cathedral,
　By sweet echoes multiplied,
Still the birds repeat the legend,
　And the name of Vogelweid.

DRINKING SONG

INSCRIPTION FOR AN ANTIQUE PITCHER

COME, old friend! sit down and listen!
　　From the pitcher, placed between us,
How the waters laugh and glisten
　In the head of old Silenus!

Old Silenus, bloated, drunken,
　Led by his inebriate Satyrs;
On his breast his head is sunken,
　Vacantly he leers and chatters.
　3*

Fauns with youthful Bacchus follow;
Ivy crowns that brow supernal
As the forehead of Apollo,
And possessing youth eternal.

Round about him, fair Bacchantes,
Bearing cymbals, flutes, and thyrses,
Wild from Naxian groves, or Zante's
Vineyards, sing delirious verses.

Thus he won, through all the nations,
Bloodless victories, and the farmer
Bore, as trophies and oblations,
Vines for banners, ploughs for armor.

Judged by no o'erzealous rigor,
Much this mystic throng expresses:
Bacchus was the type of vigor,
And Silenus of excesses.

These are ancient ethnic revels,
Of a faith long since forsaken;
Now the Satyrs, changed to devils,
Frighten mortals wine-o'ertaken.

Now to rivulets from the mountains
Point the rods of fortune-tellers;
Youth perpetual dwells in fountains, —
Not in flasks, and casks, and cellars.

Claudius, though he sang of flagons
   And huge tankards filled with Rhenish,
From that fiery blood of dragons
   Never would his own replenish.

Even Redi, though he chaunted
   Bacchus in the Tuscan valleys,
Never drank the wine he vaunted
   In his dithyrambic sallies.

Then with water fill the pitcher
   Wreathed about with classic fables;
Ne'er Falernian threw a richer
   Light upon Lucullus' tables.

Come, old friend, sit down and listen!
   As it passes thus between us,
How its wavelets laugh and glisten
   In the head of old Silenus!

THE OLD CLOCK ON THE STAIRS

L'éternité est une pendule, dont le balancier dit et redit sans cesse ces deux mots seulement, dans le silence des tombeaux : " Toujours ! jamais ! Jamais ! toujours ! "

JACQUES BRIDAINE.

SOMEWHAT back from the village street
   Stands the old-fashioned country-seat.
Across its antique portico
Tall poplar-trees their shadows throw ;
And from its station in the hall
An ancient timepiece says to all, —
      " Forever — never !
      Never — forever ! "

Half-way up the stairs it stands,
And points and beckons with its hands
From its case of massive oak,
Like a monk, who, under his cloak,
Crosses himself, and sighs, alas !
With sorrowful voice to all who pass, —
      " Forever — never !
      Never — forever ! "

By day its voice is low and light ;
But in the silent dead of night,

Distinct as a passing footstep's fall,
It echoes along the vacant hall,
Along the ceiling, along the floor,
And seems to say, at each chamber-door, —
        " Forever — never !
        Never — forever ! "

Through days of sorrow and of mirth,
Through days of death and days of birth,
Through every swift vicissitude
Of changeful time, unchanged it has stood,
And as if, like God, it all things saw,
It calmly repeats those words of awe, —
        " Forever — never !
        Never — forever ! "

In that mansion used to be
Free-hearted Hospitality ;
His great fires up the chimney roared ;
The stranger feasted at his board ;
But, like the skeleton at the feast,
That warning timepiece never ceased, —
        " Forever — never !
        Never — forever ! "

There groups of merry children played,
There youths and maidens dreaming strayed ;
O precious hours ! O golden prime,
And affluence of love and time !

Even as a miser counts his gold,
Those hours the ancient timepiece told, —
  " Forever — never !
  Never — forever ! "

From that chamber, clothed in white,
The bride came forth on her wedding night ;
There, in that silent room below,
The dead lay in his shroud of snow ;
And in the hush that followed the prayer,
Was heard the old clock on the stair, —
  " Forever — never !
  Never — forever ! "

All are scattered now and fled,
Some are married, some are dead ;
And when I ask, with throbs of pain,
" Ah ! when shall they all meet again ? "
As in the days long since gone by,
The ancient timepiece makes reply, —
  " Forever — never !
  Never — forever ! "

Never here, forever there,
Where all parting, pain, and care,
And death, and time shall disappear, —
Forever there, but never here !
The horologe of Eternity
Sayeth this incessantly, —
  " Forever — never !
  Never — forever ! "

THE ARROW AND THE SONG

I SHOT an arrow into the air,
It fell to earth, I knew not where ;
For, so swiftly it flew, the sight
Could not follow it in its flight.

I breathed a song into the air,
It fell to earth, I knew not where ;
For who has sight so keen and strong,
That it can follow the flight of song?

Long, long afterward, in an oak
I found the arrow, still unbroke ;
And the song, from beginning to end,
I found again in the heart of a friend.

SONNETS

E

THE EVENING STAR

LO! in the painted oriel of the West,
  Whose panes the sunken sun incarnadines,
  Like a fair lady at her casement, shines
  The evening star, the star of love and rest!
And then anon she doth herself divest
  Of all her radiant garments, and reclines
  Behind the sombre screen of yonder pines,
  With slumber and soft dreams of love oppressed.
O my beloved, my sweet Hesperus!
  My morning and my evening star of love!
  My best and gentlest lady! even thus,
As that fair planet in the sky above,
  Dost thou retire unto thy rest at night,
  And from thy darkened window fades the light.

AUTUMN

THOU comest, Autumn, heralded by the rain,
  With banners, by great gales incessant fanned,
  Brighter than brightest silks of Samarcand,
  And stately oxen harnessed to thy wain!
Thou standest, like imperial Charlemagne,

Upon thy bridge of gold ; thy royal hand
Outstretched with benedictions o'er the land,
Blessing the farms through all thy vast domain !
Thy shield is the red harvest moon, suspended
So long beneath the heaven's o'erhanging eaves ;
Thy steps are by the farmer's prayers attended ;
Like flames upon an altar shine the sheaves ;
And, following thee, in thy ovation splendid,
Thine almoner, the wind, scatters the golden
leaves !

DANTE

TUSCAN, that wanderest through the realms
of gloom,
With thoughtful pace, and sad, majestic eyes,
Stern thoughts and awful from thy soul arise,
Like Farinata from his fiery tomb.
Thy sacred song is like the trump of doom ;
Yet in thy heart what human sympathies,
What soft compassion glows, as in the skies
The tender stars their clouded lamps relume !
Methinks I see thee stand, with pallid cheeks,
By Fra Hilario in his diocese,
As up the convent-walls, in golden streaks,
The ascending sunbeams mark the day's decrease ;
And, as he asks what there the stranger seeks,
Thy voice along the cloister whispers, " Peace ! "

TRANSLATIONS

THE HEMLOCK TREE

FROM THE GERMAN

O HEMLOCK tree! O hemlock tree! how
   faithful are thy branches!
   Green not alone in summer time,
   But in the winter's frost and rime!
O hemlock tree! O hemlock tree! how faithful are
   thy branches!

O maiden fair! O maiden fair! how faithless is
   thy bosom!
   To love me in prosperity,
   And leave me in adversity!
O maiden fair! O maiden fair! how faithless is
   thy bosom!

The nightingale, the nightingale, thou tak'st for
   thine example!
   So long as summer laughs she sings,
   But in the autumn spreads her wings.
The nightingale, the nightingale, thou tak'st for
   thine example!

The meadow brook, the meadow brook, is mirror
    of thy falsehood!
    It flows so long as falls the rain,
    In drought its springs soon dry again.
The meadow brook, the meadow brook, is mirror
    of thy falsehood!

.

ANNIE OF THARAW

FROM THE LO'V GERMAN OF SIMON DACH

ANNIE of Tharaw, my true love of old,
    She is my life, and my goods, and my gold.

Annie of Tharaw, her heart once again
To me has surrendered in joy and in pain.

Annie of Tharaw, my riches, my good,
Thou, O my soul, my flesh and my blood!

Then come the wild weather, come sleet or come
    snow,
We will stand by each other, however it blow.

Oppression, and sickness, and sorrow, and pain
Shall be to our true love as links to the chain.

As the palm-tree standeth so straight and so tall,
The more the hail beats, and the more the rains
    fall, —

So love in our hearts shall grow mighty and strong,
Through crosses, through sorrows, through mani-
    fold wrong.

Shouldst thou be torn from me to wander alone
In a desolate land where the sun is scarce
    known, —

Through forests I 'll follow, and where the sea
    flows,
Through ice, and through iron, through armies of
    foes.

Annie of Tharaw, my light and my sun,
The threads of our two lives are woven in one.

Whate'er I have bidden thee thou hast obeyed,
Whatever forbidden thou hast not gainsaid.

How in the turmoil of life can love stand,
Where there is not one heart, and one mouth, and
    one hand?

Some seek for dissension, and trouble, and strife;
Like a dog and a cat live such man and wife.

Annie of Tharaw, such is not our love ;
Thou art my lambkin, my chick, and my dove.

Whate'er my desire is, in thine may be seen ;
I am king of the household, and thou art its queen.

It is this, O my Annie, my heart's sweetest rest,
That makes of us twain but one soul in one breast.

This turns to a heaven the hut where we dwell ;
While wrangling soon changes a home to a hell.

THE STATUE OVER THE CATHEDRAL
DOOR

FROM THE GERMAN OF JULIUS MOSEN

FORMS of saints and kings are standing
   The cathedral door above ;
Yet I saw but one among them
   Who hath soothed my soul with love.

In his mantle, — wound about him,
   As their robes the sowers wind, —
Bore he swallows and their fledglings,
   Flowers and weeds of every kind.

And so stands he calm and childlike,
  High in wind and tempest wild ;
O, were I like him exalted,
  I would be like him, a child !

And my songs, — green leaves and blossoms, —
  To the doors of heaven would bear,
Calling, even in storm and tempest,
  Round me still these birds of air.

THE LEGEND OF THE CROSSBILL

FROM THE GERMAN OF JULIUS MOSEN

ON the cross the dying Saviour
    Heavenward lifts his eyelids calm,
Feels, but scarcely feels, a trembling
  In his pierced and bleeding palm.

And by all the world forsaken,
  Sees he how with zealous care
At the ruthless nail of iron
  A little bird is striving there.

Stained with blood and never tiring,
  With its beak it doth not cease,
From the cross 't would free the Saviour,
  Its Creator's Son release.

And the Saviour speaks in mildness:
" Blest be thou of all the good !
Bear, as token of this moment,
    Marks of blood and holy rood ! "

And that bird is called the crossbill ;
    Covered all with blood so clear,
In the groves of pine it singeth
    Songs, like legends, strange to hear.

THE SEA HATH ITS PEARLS

FROM THE GERMAN OF HEINRICH HEINE

THE sea hath its pearls,
    The heaven hath its stars ;
But my heart, my heart,
    My heart hath its love.

Great are the sea and the heaven ;
    Yet greater is my heart,
And fairer than pearls and stars
    Flashes and beams my love.

Thou little, youthful maiden,
    Come unto my great heart ;
My heart, and the sea, and the heaven
    Are melting away with love !

POETIC APHORISMS

FROM THE SINNGEDICHTE OF FRIEDRICH VON LOGAU

SEVENTEENTH CENTURY

MONEY

WHEREUNTO is money good?
Who has it not wants hardihood,
Who has it has much trouble and care,
Who once has had it has despair.

THE BEST MEDICINES

Joy and Temperance and Repose
Slam the door on the doctor's nose.

SIN

MAN-LIKE is it to fall into sin,
Fiend-like is it to dwell therein,
Christ-like is it for sin to grieve,
God-like is it all sin to leave.

POVERTY AND BLINDNESS

A BLIND man is a poor man, and blind a poor
    man is ;
For the former seeth no man, and the latter no
    man sees.

LAW OF LIFE

LIVE I, so live I,
To my Lord heartily,
To my Prince faithfully,
To my Neighbor honestly.
Die I, so die I.

CREEDS

LUTHERAN, Popish, Calvinistic, all these creeds
and doctrines three
Extant are; but still the doubt is, where Chris-
tianity may be.

THE RESTLESS HEART

A MILLSTONE and the human heart are driven ever
round;
If they have nothing else to grind, they must themselves be ground.

CHRISTIAN LOVE

WHILOM Love was like a fire, and warmth and
comfort it bespoke;
But, alas! it now is quenched, and only bites us,
like the smoke.

ART AND TACT

INTELLIGENCE and courtesy not always are com-
bined ;
Often in a wooden house a golden room we find.

RETRIBUTION

THOUGH the mills of God grind slowly, yet they
grind exceeding small ;
Though with patience he stands waiting, with ex-
actness grinds he all.

TRUTH

WHEN by night the frogs are croaking, kindle but
a torch's fire,
Ha! how soon they all are silent! Thus Truth
silences the liar.

RHYMES

IF perhaps these rhymes of mine should sound not
well in strangers' ears,
They have only to bethink them that it happens so
with theirs ;
For so long as words, like mortals, call a father-
land their own,
They will be most highly valued where they are
best and longest known.

CURFEW

I.

SOLEMNLY, mournfully,
  Dealing its dole,
The Curfew Bell
  Is beginning to toll.

Cover the embers,
  And put out the light ;
Toil comes with the morning,
  And rest with the night.

Dark grow the windows,
  And quenched is the fire ;
Sound fades into silence, —
  All footsteps retire.

No voice in the chambers,
  No sound in the hall !
Sleep and oblivion
  Reign over all !

II.

THE book is completed,
    And closed, like the day;
And the hand that has written it
    Lays it away.

Dim grow its fancies;
    Forgotten they lie;
Like coals in the ashes,
    They darken and die.

Song sinks into silence,
    The story is told,
The windows are darkened,
    The hearth-stone is cold.

Darker and darker
    The black shadows fall;
Sleep and oblivion
    Reign over all.

EVANGELINE

A TALE OF ACADIE

1847

EVANGELINE

THIS is the forest primeval. The murmuring
 pines and the hemlocks,
Bearded with moss, and in garments green, indistinct in the twilight,
Stand like Druids of eld, with voices sad and prophetic,
Stand like harpers hoar, with beards that rest on
 their bosoms.
Loud from its rocky caverns, the deep-voiced neighboring ocean
Speaks, and in accents disconsolate answers the
 wail of the forest.

This is the forest primeval ; but where are the
 hearts that beneath it
Leaped like the roe, when he hears in the wood-
 land the voice of the huntsman ?
Where is the thatch-roofed village, the home of
 Acadian farmers, —
Men whose lives glided on like rivers that water
 the woodlands,

Darkened by shadows of earth, but reflecting an
    image of heaven ?
Waste are those pleasant farms, and the farmers
    forever departed !
Scattered like dust and leaves, when the mighty
    blasts of October
Seize them, and whirl them aloft, and sprinkle
    them far o'er the ocean.
Naught but tradition remains of the beautiful vil-
    lage of Grand-Pré.

  Ye who believe in affection that hopes, and en-
    dures, and is patient,
Ye who believe in the beauty and strength of
    woman's devotion,
List to the mournful tradition still sung by the
    pines of the forest ;
List to a Tale of Love in Acadie, home of the
    happy.

PART THE FIRST

I.

IN the Acadian land, on the shores of the Basin
    of Minas,
Distant, secluded, still, the little village of Grand-
    Pré
Lay in the fruitful valley. Vast meadows stretched
    to the eastward,
Giving the village its name, and pasture to flocks
    without number.
Dikes, that the hands of the farmers had raised
    with labor incessant,
Shut out the turbulent tides; but at stated sea-
    sons the flood-gates
Opened, and welcomed the sea to wander at will
    o'er the meadows.
West and south there were fields of flax, and
    orchards and cornfields
Spreading afar and unfenced o'er the plain; and
    away to the northward
Blomidon rose, and the forests old, and aloft on
    the mountains

Sea-fogs pitched their tents, and mists from the
    mighty Atlantic
Looked on the happy valley, but ne'er from their
    station descended.
There, in the midst of its farms, reposed the Aca-
    dian village.
Strongly built were the houses, with frames of oak
    and of chestnut,
Such as the peasants of Normandy built in the
    reign of the Henries.
Thatched were the roofs, with dormer-windows;
    and gables projecting
Over the basement below protected and shaded
    the door-way.
There in the tranquil evenings of summer, when
    brightly the sunset
Lighted the village street, and gilded the vanes
    on the chimneys,
Matrons and maidens sat in snow-white caps and
    in kirtles
Scarlet and blue and green, with distaffs spinning
    the golden
Flax for the gossiping looms, whose noisy shuttles
    within doors
Mingled their sound with the whir of the wheels
    and the songs of the maidens.
Solemnly down the street came the parish priest,
    and the children
Paused in their play to kiss the hand he extended
    to bless them.

Reverend walked he among them; and up rose
    matrons and maidens,
Hailing his slow approach with words of affection-
    ate welcome.
Then came the laborers home from the field, and
    serenely the sun sank
Down to his rest, and twilight prevailed. Anon
    from the belfry
Softly the Angelus sounded, and over the roofs of
    the village
Columns of pale blue smoke, like clouds of incense
    ascending,
Rose from a hundred hearths, the homes of peace
    and contentment.
Thus dwelt together in love these simple Acadian
    farmers, —
Dwelt in the love of God and of man. Alike
    were they free from
Fear, that reigns with the tyrant, and envy, the
    vice of republics.
Neither locks had they to their doors, nor bars to
    their windows;
But their dwellings were open as day and the
    hearts of the owners;
There the richest was poor, and the poorest lived
    in abundance.

    Somewhat apart from the village, and nearer
    the Basin of Minas,

Benedict Bellefontaine, the wealthiest farmer of
    Grand-Pré,
Dwelt on his goodly acres ; and with him, direct-
    ing his household,
Gentle Evangeline lived, his child, and the pride
    of the village.
Stalworth and stately in form was the man of sev-
    enty winters ;
Hearty and hale was he, an oak that is covered
    with snow-flakes ;
White as the snow were his locks, and his cheeks
    as brown as the oak-leaves.
Fair was she to behold, that maiden of seventeen
    summers.
Black were her eyes as the berry that grows on
    the thorn by the wayside,
Black, yet how softly they gleamed beneath the
    brown shade of her tresses !
Sweet was her breath as the breath of kine that
    feed in the meadows.
When in the harvest heat she bore to the reapers
    at noontide
Flagons of home-brewed ale, ah ! fair in sooth was
    the maiden.
Fairer was she when, on Sunday morn, while the
    bell from its turret
Sprinkled with holy sounds the air, as the priest
    with his hyssop
Sprinkles the congregation, and scatters blessings
    upon them,

Down the long street she passed, with her chaplet
    of beads and her missal,
Wearing her Norman cap, and her kirtle of blue,
    and the ear-rings,
Brought in the olden time from France, and since,
    as an heirloom,
Handed down from mother to child, through long
    generations.
But a celestial brightness — a more ethereal beau-
    ty —
Shone on her face and encircled her form, when,
    after confession,
Homeward serenely she walked with God's bene-
    diction upon her.
When she had passed, it seemed like the ceasing
    of exquisite music.

Firmly builded with rafters of oak, the house of
    the farmer
Stood on the side of a hill commanding the sea ;
    and a shady
Sycamore grew by the door, with a woodbine
    wreathing around it.
Rudely carved was the porch, with seats beneath ;
    and a footpath
Led through an orchard wide, and disappeared in
    the meadow.
Under the sycamore-tree were hives overhung by
    a penthouse,

Such as the traveller sees in regions remote by the
    roadside,
Built o'er a box for the poor, or the blessed image
    of Mary.
Farther down, on the slope of the hill, was the
    well with its moss-grown
Bucket, fastened with iron, and near it a trough
    for the horses.
Shielding the house from storms, on the north,
    were the barns and the farm-yard,
There stood the broad-wheeled wains and the
    antique ploughs and the harrows ;
There were the folds for the sheep ; and there,
    in his feathered seraglio,
Strutted the lordly turkey, and crowed the cock,
    with the selfsame
Voice that in ages of old had startled the penitent
    Peter.
Bursting with hay were the barns, themselves a
    village.   In each one
Far o'er the gable projected a roof of thatch ; and
    a staircase,
Under the sheltering eaves, led up to the odorous
    corn-loft.
There too the dove-cot stood, with its meek and
    innocent inmates
Murmuring ever of love ; while above in the vari-
    ant breezes
Numberless noisy weathercocks rattled and sang
    of mutation.

Thus, at peace with God and the world, the
    farmer of Grand-Pré
Lived on his sunny farm, and Evangeline governed
    his household.
Many a youth, as he knelt in the church and
    opened his missal,
Fixed his eyes upon her, as the saint of his deepest
    devotion ;
Happy was he who might touch her hand or the
    hem of her garment !
Many a suitor came to her door, by the darkness
    befriended,
And, as he knocked and waited to hear the sound
    of her footsteps,
Knew not which beat the louder, his heart or the
    knocker of iron ;
Or at the joyous feast of the Patron Saint of the
    village,
Bolder grew, and pressed her hand in the dance as
    he whispered
Hurried words of love, that seemed a part of the
    music.
But, among all who came, young Gabriel only was
    welcome ;
Gabriel Lajeunesse, the son of Basil the black-
    smith,
Who was a mighty man in the village, and honored
    of all men ;
For, since the birth of time, throughout all ages
    and nations,

Has the craft of the smith been held in repute by
  the people.
Basil was Benedict's friend. Their children from
  earliest childhood
Grew up together as brother and sister; and
  Father Felician,
Priest and pedagogue both in the village, had
  taught them their letters
Out of the selfsame book, with the hymns of the
  church and the plain-song.
But when the hymn was sung, and the daily lesson
  completed,
Swiftly they hurried away to the forge of Basil the
  blacksmith.
There at the door they stood, with wondering eyes
  to behold him
Take in his leathern lap the hoof of the horse as
  a plaything,
Nailing the shoe in its place; while near him the
  tire of the cart-wheel
Lay like a fiery snake, coiled round in a circle of
  cinders.
Oft on autumnal eves, when without in the gathering darkness
Bursting with light seemed the smithy, through
  every cranny and crevice,
Warm by the forge within they watched the laboring bellows,
And as its panting ceased, and the sparks expired
  in the ashes,

Merrily laughed, and said they were nuns going
    into the chapel.
Oft on sledges in winter, as swift as the swoop of
    the eagle,
Down the hillside bounding, they glided away o'er
    the meadow.
Oft in the barns they climbed to the populous nests
    on the rafters,
Seeking with eager eyes that wondrous stone,
    which the swallow
Brings from the shore of the sea to restore the
    sight of its fledglings ;
Lucky was he who found that stone in the nest of
    the swallow !
Thus passed a few swift years, and they no longer
    were children.
He was a valiant youth, and his face, like the face
    of the morning,
Gladdened the earth with its light, and ripened
    thought into action.
She was a woman now, with the heart and hopes
    of a woman.
"Sunshine of Saint Eulalie" was she called ; for
    that was the sunshine
Which, as the farmers believed, would load their
    orchards with apples ;
She, too, would bring to her husband's house
    delight and abundance,
Filling it full of love and the ruddy faces of children.

II.

Now had the season returned, when the nights
    grow colder and longer,
And the retreating sun the sign of the Scorpion
    enters.
Birds of passage sailed through the leaden air,
    from the ice-bound,
Desolate northern bays to the shores of tropical
    islands.
Harvests were gathered in; and wild with the
    winds of September
Wrestled the trees of the forest, as Jacob of old
    with the angel.
All the signs foretold a winter long and inclem-
    ent.
Bees, with prophetic instinct of want, had hoarded
    their honey
Till the hives overflowed; and the Indian hunters
    asserted
Cold would the winter be, for thick was the fur of
    the foxes.
Such was the advent of autumn. Then followed
    that beautiful season,
Called by the pious Acadian peasants the Summer
    of All-Saints !

Filled was the air with a dreamy and magical light ;
and the landscape
Lay as if new-created in all the freshness of childhood.
Peace seemed to reign upon earth, and the restless
heart of the ocean
Was for a moment consoled.   All sounds were in
harmony blended.
Voices of children at play, the crowing of cocks in
the farm-yards,
Whir of wings in the drowsy air, and the cooing
of pigeons,
All were subdued and low as the murmurs of love,
and the great sun
Looked with the eye of love through the golden
vapors around him ;
While arrayed in its robes of russet and scarlet
and yellow,
Bright with the sheen of the dew, each glittering
tree of the forest
Flashed like the plane-tree the Persian adorned
with mantles and jewels.

Now recommenced the reign of rest and affection and stillness.
Day with its burden and heat had departed, and
twilight descending
Brought back the evening star to the sky, and the
herds to the homestead.

Pawing the ground they came, and resting their
    necks on each other,
And with their nostrils distended inhaling the
    freshness of evening.
Foremost, bearing the bell, Evangeline's beautiful
    heifer,
Proud of her snow-white hide, and the ribbon that
    waved from her collar,
Quietly paced and slow, as if conscious of human
    affection.
Then came the shepherd back with his bleating
    flocks from the seaside,
Where was their favorite pasture. Behind them
    followed the watch-dog,
Patient, full of importance, and grand in the pride
    of his instinct,
Walking from side to side with a lordly air, and
    superbly
Waving his bushy tail, and urging forward the
    stragglers ;
Regent of flocks was he when the shepherd slept ;
    their protector,
When from the forest at night, through the starry
    silence, the wolves howled.
Late, with the rising moon, returned the wains
    from the marshes,
Laden with briny hay, that filled the air with its
    odor.
Cheerily neighed the steeds, with dew on their
    manes and their fetlocks,

While aloft on their shoulders the wooden and
 ponderous saddles,
Painted with brilliant dyes, and adorned with
 tassels of crimson,
Nodded in bright array, like hollyhocks heavy with
 blossoms.
Patiently stood the cows meanwhile, and yielded
 their udders
Unto the milkmaid's hand; whilst loud and in
 regular cadence
Into the sounding pails the foaming streamlets
 descended.
Lowing of cattle and peals of laughter were heard
 in the farm-yard,
Echoed back by the barns. Anon they sank into
 stillness ;
Heavily closed, with a jarring sound, the valves of
 the barn-doors,
Rattled the wooden bars, and all for a season was
 silent.

In-doors, warm by the wide-mouthed fireplace,
 idly the farmer
Sat in his elbow-chair, and watched how the flames
 and the smoke-wreaths
Struggled together like foes in a burning city.
 Behind him,
Nodding and mocking along the wall, with ges-
 tures fantastic,

Darted his own huge shadow, and vanished away
    into darkness.
Faces, clumsily carved in oak, on the back of his
    arm-chair
Laughed in the flickering light, and the pewter
    plates on the dresser
Caught and reflected the flame, as shields of armies
    the sunshine.
Fragments of song the old man sang, and carols of
    Christmas,
Such as at home, in the olden time, his fathers
    before him
Sang in their Norman orchards and bright Bur-
    gundian vineyards.
Close at her father's side was the gentle Evan-
    geline seated,
Spinning flax for the loom, that stood in the corner
    behind her.
Silent awhile were its treadles, at rest was its
    diligent shuttle,
While the monotonous drone of the wheel, like the
    drone of a bagpipe,
Followed the old man's song, and united the frag-
    ments together.
As in a church, when the chant of the choir at
    intervals ceases,
Footfalls are heard in the aisles, or words of the
    priest at the altar,
So, in each pause of the song, with measured
    motion the clock clicked.

Thus as they sat, there were footsteps heard,
    and, suddenly lifted,
Sounded the wooden latch, and the door swung
    back on its hinges.
Benedict knew by the hob-nailed shoes it was
    Basil the blacksmith,
And by her beating heart Evangeline knew who
    was with him.
"Welcome!" the farmer exclaimed, as their foot-
    steps paused on the threshold,
"Welcome, Basil, my friend! Come, take thy
    place on the settle
Close by the chimney-side, which is always empty
    without thee ;
Take from the shelf overhead thy pipe and the box
    of tobacco ;
Never so much thyself art thou as when through
    the curling
Smoke of the pipe or the forge thy friendly and
    jovial face gleams
Round and red as the harvest moon through the
    mist of the marshes."
Then, with a smile of content, thus answered Basil
    the blacksmith,
Taking with easy air the accustomed seat by the
    fireside : —
"Benedict Bellefontaine, thou hast ever thy jest
    and thy ballad !
Ever in cheerfullest mood art thou, when others are
    filled with

Gloomy forebodings of ill, and see only ruin before
   them.
Happy art thou, as if every day thou hadst picked
   up a horseshoe."
Pausing a moment, to take the pipe that Evange-
   line brought him,
And with a coal from the embers had lighted, he
   slowly continued : —
"Four days now are passed since the English
   ships at their anchors
Ride in the Gaspereau's mouth, with their cannon
   pointed against us.
What their design may be is unknown ; but all are
   commanded
On the morrow to meet in the church, where his
   Majesty's mandate
Will be proclaimed as law in the land.   Alas ! in
   the mean time
Many surmises of evil alarm the hearts of the
   people."
Then made answer the farmer : — "Perhaps some
   friendlier purpose
Brings these ships to our shores.   Perhaps the
   harvests in England
By untimely rains or untimelier heat have been
   blighted,
And from our bursting barns they would feed their
   cattle and children."
"Not so thinketh the folk in the village," said,
   warmly, the blacksmith,

Shaking his head, as in doubt; then, heaving a
    sigh, he continued : —
"Louisburg is not forgotten, nor Beau Séjour, nor
    Port Royal.
Many already have fled to the forest, and lurk on
    its outskirts,
Waiting with anxious hearts the dubious fate of
    to-morrow.
Arms have been taken from us, and warlike weap-
    ons of all kinds ;
Nothing is left but the blacksmith's sledge and the
    scythe of the mower."
Then with a pleasant smile made answer the jovial
    farmer : —
"Safer are we unarmed, in the midst of our flocks
    and our cornfields,
Safer within these peaceful dikes, besieged by the
    ocean,
Than our fathers in forts, besieged by the enemy's
    cannon.
Fear no evil, my friend, and to-night may no
    shadow of sorrow
Fall on this house and hearth; for this is the
    night of the contract.
Built are the house and the barn. The merry lads
    of the village
Strongly have built them and well ; and, breaking
    the glebe round about them,
Filled the barn with hay, and the house with food
    for a twelvemonth.

5*

René Leblanc will be here anon, with his papers
    and inkhorn.
Shall we not then be glad, and rejoice in the joy
    of our children?"
As apart by the window she stood, with her hand
    in her lover's,
Blushing Evangeline heard the words that her
    father had spoken,
And, as they died on his lips, the worthy notary
    entered.

III.

BENT like a laboring oar, that toils in the surf of
    the ocean,
Bent, but not broken, by age was the form of the
    notary public;
Shocks of yellow hair, like the silken floss of the
    maize, hung
Over his shoulders; his forehead was high; and
    glasses with horn bows
Sat astride on his nose, with a look of wisdom
    supernal.
Father of twenty children was he, and more than a
    hundred
Children's children rode on his knee, and heard
    his great watch tick.

Four long years in the times of the war had he lan-
    guished a captive,
Suffering much in an old French fort as the friend
    of the English.
Now, though warier grown, without all guile or sus-
    picion,
Ripe in wisdom was he, but patient, and simple,
    and childlike.
He was beloved by all, and most of all by the chil-
    dren ;
For he told them tales of the Loup-garou in the
    forest,
And of the goblin that came in the night to water
    the horses,
And of the white Létiche, the ghost of a child who
    unchristened
Died, and was doomed to haunt unseen the cham-
    bers of children ;
And how on Christmas eve the oxen talked in the
    stable,
And how the fever was cured by a spider shut up
    in a nutshell,
And of the marvellous powers of four-leaved clover
    and norseshoes,
With whatsoever else was writ in the lore of the
    village.
Then up rose from his seat by the fireside Basil
    the blacksmith,
Knocked from his pipe the ashes, and slowly ex-
    tending his right hand,

"Father Leblanc," he exclaimed, "thou hast heard
    the talk in the village,
And, perchance, canst tell us some news of these
    ships and their errand."
Then with modest demeanor made answer the no-
    tary public, —
"Gossip enough have I heard, in sooth, yet am
    never the wiser;
And what their errand may be I know not better
    than others.
Yet am I not of those who imagine some evil inten-
    tion
Brings them here, for we are at peace; and why
    then molest us?"
"God's name!" shouted the hasty and somewhat
    irascible blacksmith;
"Must we in all things look for the how, and the
    why, and the wherefore?
Daily injustice is done, and might is the right of
    the strongest!"
But, without heeding his warmth, continued the
    notary public, —
"Man is unjust, but God is just; and finally jus-
    tice
Triumphs; and well I remember a story, that often
    consoled me,
When as a captive I lay in the old French fort at
    Port Royal."
This was the old man's favorite tale, and he loved
    to repeat it

When his neighbors complained that any injustice
was done them.
" Once in an ancient city, whose name I no longer
remember,
Raised aloft on a column, a brazen statue of Justice
Stood in the public square, upholding the scales in
its left hand,
And in its right a sword, as an emblem that justice
presided
Over the laws of the land, and the hearts and
homes of the people.
Even the birds had built their nests in the scales
of the balance,
Having no fear of the sword that flashed in the
sunshine above them.
But in the course of time the laws of the land were
corrupted ;
Might took the place of right, and the weak were
oppressed, and the mighty
Ruled with an iron rod. Then it chanced in a
nobleman's palace
That a necklace of pearls was lost, and erelong a
suspicion
Fell on an orphan girl who lived as maid in the
household.
She, after form of trial condemned to die on the
scaffold,
Patiently met her doom at the foot of the statue of
Justice.

As to her Father in heaven her innocent spirit
    ascended,
Lo! o'er the city a tempest rose; and the bolts of
    the thunder
Smote the statue of bronze, and hurled in wrath
    from its left hand
Down on the pavement below the clattering scales
    of the balance,
And in the hollow thereof was found the nest of a
    magpie,
Into whose clay-built walls the necklace of pearls
    was inwoven."
Silenced, but not convinced, when the story was
    ended, the blacksmith
Stood like a man who fain would speak, but findeth
    no language;
All his thoughts were congealed into lines on his
    face, as the vapors
Freeze in fantastic shapes on the window-panes
    in the winter.

   Then Evangeline lighted the brazen lamp on the
    table,
Filled, till it overflowed, the pewter tankard with
    home-brewed
Nut-brown ale, that was famed for its strength in
    the village of Grand-Pré;
While from his pocket the notary drew his papers
    and inkhorn,

Wrote with a steady hand the date and the age of
the parties,

Naming the dower of the bride in flocks of sheep
and in cattle.

Orderly all things proceeded, and duly and well
were completed,

And the great seal of the law was set like a sun on
the margin.

Then from his leathern pouch the farmer threw on
the table

Three times the old man's fee in solid pieces of
silver ;

And the notary rising, and blessing the bride and
the bridegroom,

Lifted aloft the tankard of ale and drank to their
welfare.

Wiping the foam from his lip, he solemnly bowed
and departed,

While in silence the others sat and mused by the
fireside,

Till Evangeline brought the draught-board out of
its corner.

Soon was the game begun.   In friendly contention
the old men

Laughed at each lucky hit, or unsuccessful ma-
nœuvre,

Laughed when a man was crowned, or a breach
was made in the king-row.

Meanwhile apart, in the twilight gloom of a window's embrasure,

Sat the lovers, and whispered together, beholding
    the moon rise

Over the pallid sea and the silvery mist of the
    meadows.

Silently one by one, in the infinite meadows of
    heaven,

Blossomed the lovely stars, the forget-me-nots of
    the angels.

Thus was the evening passed. Anon the bell
    from the belfry

Rang out the hour of nine, the village curfew, and
    straightway

Rose the guests and departed ; and silence reigned
    in the household.

Many a farewell word and sweet good-night on the
    door-step

Lingered long in Evangeline's heart, and filled it
    with gladness.

Carefully then were covered the embers that glowed
    on the hearth-stone,

And on the oaken stairs resounded the tread of the
    farmer.

Soon with a soundless step the foot of Evangeline
    followed.

Up the staircase moved a luminous space in the
    darkness,

Lighted less by the lamp than the shining face of
    the maiden.

Silent she passed the hall, and entered the door of
    her chamber.
Simple that chamber was, with its curtains of
    white, and its clothes-press
Ample and high, on whose spacious shelves were
    carefully folded
Linen and woollen stuffs, by the hand of Evangeline
    woven.
This was the precious dower she would bring to
    her husband in marriage,
Better than flocks and herds, being proofs of her
    skill as a housewife.
Soon she extinguished her lamp, for the mellow
    and radiant moonlight
Streamed through the windows, and lighted the
    room, till the heart of the maiden
Swelled and obeyed its power, like the tremulous
    tides of the ocean.
Ah! she was fair, exceeding fair to behold, as she
    stood with
Naked snow-white feet on the gleaming floor of her
    chamber!
Little she dreamed that below, among the trees of
    the orchard,
Waited her lover and watched for the gleam of her
    lamp and her shadow.
Yet were her thoughts of him, and at times a feel-
    ing of sadness
Passed o'er her soul, as the sailing shade of clouds
    in the moonlight

Flitted across the floor and darkened the room for
    a moment.
And, as she gazed from the window, she saw se-
    renely the moon pass
Forth from the folds of a cloud, and one star fol-
    low her footsteps,
As out of Abraham's tent young Ishmael wandered
    with Hagar!

I·V.

PLEASANTLY rose next morn the sun on the village
    of Grand-Pré.
Pleasantly gleamed in the soft, sweet air the Basin
    of Minas,
Where the ships, with their wavering shadows, were
    riding at anchor.
Life had long been astir in the village, and clamor-
    ous labor
Knocked with its hundred hands at the golden
    gates of the morning.
Now from the country around, from the farms and
    neighboring hamlets,
Came in their holiday dresses the blithe Acadian
    peasants.
Many a glad good-morrow and jocund laugh from
    the young folk

Made the bright air brighter, as up from the numerous meadows,
Where no path could be seen but the track of wheels in the greensward,
Group after group appeared, and joined, or passed on the highway.
Long ere noon, in the village all sounds of labor were silenced.
Thronged were the streets with people ; and noisy groups at the house-doors
Sat in the cheerful sun, and rejoiced and gossiped together.
Every house was an inn, where all were welcomed and feasted ;
For with this simple people, who lived like brothers together,
All things were held in common, and what one had was another's.
Yet under Benedict's roof hospitality seemed more abundant. :
For Evangeline stood among the guests of her father ;
Bright was her face with smiles, and words of welcome and gladness
Fell from her beautiful lips, and blessed the cup as she gave it.

Under the open sky, in the odorous air of the orchard,

Stript of its golden fruit, was spread the feast of
    betrothal.

There in the shade of the porch were the priest and
    the notary seated ;

There good Benedict sat, and sturdy Basil the
    blacksmith.

Not far withdrawn from these, by the cider-press
    and the beehives,

Michael the fiddler was placed, with the gayest of
    hearts and of waistcoats.

Shadow and light from the leaves alternately
    played on his snow-white

Hair, as it waved in the wind ; and the jolly face
    of the fiddler

Glowed like a living coal when the ashes are blown
    from the embers.

Gayly the old man sang to the vibrant sound of his
    fiddle,

Tous les Bourgeois de Chartres, and *Le Carillon de
    Dunkerque*,

And anon with his wooden shoes beat time to the
    music.

Merrily, merrily whirled the wheels of the dizzying
    dances

Under the orchard-trees and down the path to the
    meadows ;

Old folk and young together, and children min-
    gled among them.

Fairest of all the maids was Evangeline, Benedict's
    daughter !

Noblest of all the youths was Gabriel, son of the
blacksmith!

So passed the morning away. And lo! with a
summons sonorous
Sounded the bell from its tower, and over the
meadows a drum beat.
Thronged erelong was the church with men. Without, in the churchyard,·
Waited the women. They stood by the graves,
and hung on the headstones
Garlands of autumn-leaves and evergreens fresh
from the forest.
Then came the guard from the ships, and marching
proudly among them
Entered the sacred portal. With loud and disso-
nant clangor
Echoed the sound of their brazen drums from ceil-
ing and casement, —
Echoed a moment only, and slowly the ponderous
portal
Closed, and in silence the crowd awaited the will
of the soldiers.
Then uprose their commander, and spake from the
steps of the altar,
Holding aloft in his hands, with its seals, the royal
commission.
"You are convened this day," he said, "by his
Majesty's orders.

Clement and kind has he been ; but how you have
  answered his kindness,
Let your own hearts reply ! To my natural make
  and my temper
Painful the task is I do, which to you I know must
  be grievous.
Yet must I bow and obey, and deliver the will of
  our monarch ;
Namely, that all your lands, and dwellings, and cattle of all kinds
Forfeited be to the crown ; and that you yourselves
  from this province
Be transported to other lands. God grant you may
  . dwell there
Ever as faithful subjects, a happy and peaceable
  people !
Prisoners now I declare you ; for such is his Majesty's pleasure ! "
As, when the air is serene in the sultry solstice of
  summer,
Suddenly gathers a storm, and the deadly sling of
  the hailstones
Beats down the farmer's corn in the field and shat-
  ters his windows,
Hiding the sun, and strewing the ground with
  thatch from the house-roofs,
Bellowing fly the herds, and seek to break their en-
  closures ;
So on the hearts of the people descended the words
  of the speaker.

Silent a moment they stood in speechless wonder,
   and then rose

Louder and ever louder a wail of sorrow and anger,

And, by one impulse moved, they madly rushed to
   the door-way.

Vain was the hope of escape ; and cries and fierce
   imprecations

Rang through the house of prayer ; and high o'er
   the heads of the others

Rose, with his arms uplifted, the figure of Basil the
   blacksmith,

As, on a stormy sea, a spar is tossed by the bil-
   lows.

Flushed was his face and distorted with passion ;
   and wildly he shouted, —

"Down with the tyrants of England ! we never
   have sworn them allegiance !

Death to these foreign soldiers, who seize on our
   homes and our harvests ! "

More he fain would have said, but the merciless
   hand of a soldier

Smote him upon the mouth, and dragged him down
   to the pavement.

In the midst of the strife and tumult of angry
   contention,

Lo ! the door of the chancel opened, and Father
   Felician

Entered, with serious mien, and ascended the steps
    of the altar.

Raising his reverend hand, with a gesture he awed
    into silence

All that clamorous throng; and thus he spake to
    his people;

Deep were his tones and solemn; in accents meas-
    ured and mournful

Spake he, as, after the tocsin's alarum, distinctly
    the clock strikes.

"What is this that ye do, my children? what mad-
    ness has seized you?

Forty years of my life have I labored among you,
    and taught you,

Not in word alone, but in deed, to love one
    another!

Is this the fruit of my toils, of my vigils and prayers
    and privations?

Have you so soon forgotten all lessons of love and
    forgiveness?

This is the house of the Prince of Peace, and would
    you profane it

Thus with violent deeds and hearts overflowing
    with hatred?

Lo! where the crucified Christ from his cross is
    gazing upon you!

See! in those sorrowful eyes what meekness and
    holy compassion!

Hark! how those lips still repeat the prayer, 'O
    Father, forgive them!'

Let us repeat that prayer in the hour when the
    wicked assail us,
Let us repeat it now, and say, ' O Father, forgive
    them ! ' "
Few were his words of rebuke, but deep in the
    hearts of his people
Sank they, and sobs of contrition succeeded the
    passionate outbreak,
While they repeated his prayer, and said, " O Fa-
    ther, forgive them ! "

Then came the evening service. The tapers
    gleamed from the altar.
Fervent and deep was the voice of the priest, and
    the people responded,
Not with their lips alone, but their hearts ; and the
    Ave Maria
Sang they, and fell on their knees, and their souls,
    with devotion translated,
Rose on the ardor of prayer, like Elijah ascending
    to heaven.

Meanwhile had spread in the village the tidings
    of ill, and on all sides
Wandered, wailing, from house to house the women
    and children.
Long at her father's door Evangeline stood, with
    her right hand
Shielding her eyes from the level rays of the sun,
    that, descending,

Lighted the village street with mysterious splendor,
and roofed each

Peasant's cottage with golden thatch, and embla-
zoned its windows.

Long within had been spread the snow-white cloth
on the table ;

There stood the wheaten loaf, and the honey fragrant with wild-flowers ;

There stood the tankard of ale, and the cheese
fresh brought from the dairy ;

And, at the head of the board, the great arm-chair
of the farmer.

Thus did Evangeline wait at her father's door, as
the sunset

Threw the long shadows of trees o'er the broad
ambrosial meadows.

Ah ! on her spirit within a deeper shadow had
fallen,

And from the fields of her soul a fragrance celestial
ascended, —

Charity, meekness, love, and hope, and forgiveness,
and patience !

Then, all-forgetful of self, she wandered into the
village,

Cheering with looks and words the mournful hearts
of the women,

As o'er the darkening fields with lingering steps
they departed.

Urged by their household cares, and the weary feet
of their children.

Down sank the great red sun, and in golden, glim-
mering vapors
Veiled the light of his face, like the Prophet descending from Sinai.
Sweetly over the village the bell of the Angelus
sounded.

Meanwhile, amid the gloom, by the church Evangeline lingered.
All was silent within ; and in vain at the door and
the windows
Stood she, and listened and looked, till, overcome
by emotion,
"Gabriel !" cried she aloud with tremulous voice ;
but no answer
Came from the graves of the dead, nor the gloomier
grave of the living.
Slowly at length she returned to the tenantless
house of her father.
Smouldered the fire on the hearth, on the board
was the supper untasted,
Empty and drear was each room, and haunted with
phantoms of terror.
Sadly echoed her step on the stair and the floor of
her chamber.
In the dead of the night she heard the disconsolate
rain fall
Loud on the withered leaves of the sycamore-tree
by the window.

Keenly the lightning flashed ; and the voice of the
    echoing thunder
Told her that God was in heaven, and governed
    the world he created !
Then she remembered the tale she had heard of
    the justice of Heaven ;
Soothed was her troubled soul, and she peacefully
    slumbered till morning.

V.

FOUR times the sun had risen and set ; and now
    on the fifth day
Cheerily called the cock to the sleeping maids of
    the farm-house.
Soon o'er the yellow fields, in silent and mournful
    procession,
Came from the neighboring hamlets and farms the
    Acadian women,
Driving in ponderous wains their household goods
    to the sea-shore,
Pausing and looking back to gaze once more on
    their dwellings,
Ere they were shut from sight by the winding road
    and the woodland.
Close at their sides their children ran, and urged
    on the oxen,

While in their little hands they clasped some fragments of playthings.

Thus to the Gaspereau's mouth they hurried;
and there on the sea-beach
Piled in confusion lay the household goods of the
peasants.
All day long between the shore and the ships did
the boats ply;
All day long the wains came laboring down from
the village.
Late in the afternoon, when the sun was near to his
setting,
Echoed far o'er the fields came the roll of drums
from the churchyard.
Thither the women and children thronged. On a
sudden the church-doors
Opened, and forth came the guard, and marching
in gloomy procession
Followed the long-imprisoned, but patient, Acadian
farmers.
Even as pilgrims, who journey afar from their
homes and their country,
Sing as they go, and in singing forget they are
weary and wayworn,
So with songs on their lips the Acadian peasants
descended
Down from the church to the shore, amid their
wives and their daughters.

Foremost the young men came ; and, raising togeth-
er their voices,
Sang with tremulous lips a chant of the Catholic
Missions : —
"Sacred heart of the Saviour! O inexhaustible
fountain !
Fill our hearts this day with strength and submis-
sion and patience !"
Then the old men, as they marched, and the
women that stood by the wayside
Joined in the sacred psalm, and the birds in the
sunshine above them
Mingled their notes therewith, like voices of spirits
departed.

Half-way down to the shore Evangeline waited
in silence,
Not overcome with grief, but strong in the hour of
affliction, —
Calmly and sadly she waited, until the procession
approached her,
And she beheld the face of Gabriel pale with emotion.
Tears then filled her eyes, and, eagerly running to
meet him,
Clasped she his hands, and laid her head on his
shoulder, and whispered, —
"Gabriel! be of good cheer! for if we love one
another,

Nothing, in truth, can harm us, whatever mis-
    chances may happen ! "
Smiling she spake these words ; then suddenly
    paused, for her father
Saw she slowly advancing. Alas ! how changed
    was his aspect !
Gone was the glow from his cheek, and the fire
    from his eye, and his footstep
Heavier seemed with the weight of the heavy heart
    in his bosom.
But with a smile and a sigh, she clasped his neck
    and embraced him,
Speaking words of endearment where words of
    comfort availed not.
Thus to the Gaspereau's mouth moved on that
    mournful procession.

There disorder prevailed, and the tumult and stir
    of embarking.
Busily plied the freighted boats ; and in the confu-
    sion
Wives were torn from their husbands, and mothers,
    too late, saw their children
Left on the land, extending their arms, with wildest
    entreaties.
So unto separate ships were Basil and Gabriel car-
    ried,
While in despair on the shore Evangeline stood
    with her father.

Half the task was not done when the sun went
    down, and the twilight

Deepened and darkenèd around ; and in haste the
    refluent ocean

Fled away from the shore, and left the line of the
    sand-beach

Covered with waifs of the tide, with kelp and the
    slippery sea-weed.

Farther back in the midst of the household goods
    and the wagons,

Like to a gypsy camp, or a leaguer after a bat-
    tle,

All escape cut off by the sea, and the sentinels
    near them,

Lay encamped for the night the houseless Acadian
    farmers.

Back to its nethermost caves retreated the bellow-
    ing ocean,

Dragging adown the beach the rattling pebbles,
    and leaving

Inland and far up the shore the stranded boats of
    the sailors.

Then, as the night descended, the herds returned
    from their pastures ;

Sweet was the moist still air with the odor of milk
    from their udders ;

Lowing they waited, and long, at the well-known
    bars of the farm-yard, —

Waited and looked in vain for the voice and the
    hand of the milkmaid.

Silence reigned in the streets ; from the church no
    Angelus sounded,
Rose no smoke from the roofs, and gleamed no
    lights from the windows.

But on the shores meanwhile the evening fires
    had been kindled,
Built of the drift-wood thrown on the sands from
    wrecks in the tempest.
Round them shapes of gloom and sorrowful faces
    were gathered,
Voices of women were heard, and of men, and the
    crying of children.
Onward from fire to fire, as from hearth to hearth
    in his parish,
Wandered the faithful priest, consoling and bless-
    ing and cheering,
Like unto shipwrecked Paul on Melita's desolate
    sea-shore.
Thus he approached the place where Evangeline
    sat with her father,
And in the flickering light beheld the face of the
    old man,
Haggard and hollow and wan, and without either
    thought or emotion,
E'en as the face of a clock from which the hands
    have been taken.
Vainly Evangeline strove with words and caresses
    to cheer him,

Vainly offered him food; yet he moved not, he
    looked not, he spake not,
But, with a vacant stare, ever gazed at the flicker-
    ing fire-light.
"*Benedicite!*" murmured the priest, in tones of
    compassion.
More he fain would have said, but his heart was
    full, and his accents
Faltered and paused on his lips, as the feet of a
    child on a threshold,
Hushed by the scene he beholds, and the awful
    presence of sorrow.
Silently, therefore, he laid his hand on the head of
    the maiden,
Raising his tearful eyes to the silent stars that
    above them
Moved on their way, unperturbed by the wrongs
    and sorrows of mortals.
Then sat he down at her side, and they wept to-
    gether in silence.

    Suddenly rose from the south a light, as in au-
    tumn the blood-red
Moon climbs the crystal walls of heaven, and o'er
    the horizon
Titan-like stretches its hundred hands upon moun-
    tain and meadow,
Seizing the rocks and the rivers, and piling huge
    shadows together.

Broader and ever broader it gleamed on the roofs
    of the village,
Gleamed on the sky and the sea, and the ships that
    lay in the roadstead.
Columns of shining smoke uprose, and flashes of
    flame were
Thrust through their folds and withdrawn, like the
    quivering hands of a martyr.
Then as the wind seized the gleeds and the burn-
    ing thatch, and, uplifting,
Whirled them aloft through the air, at once from a
    hundred house-tops
Started the sheeted smoke with flashes of flame in-
    termingled.

    These things beheld in dismay the crowd on the
    shore and on shipboard.
Speechless at first they stood, then cried aloud in
    their anguish,
" We shall behold no more our homes in the village
    of Grand-Pré ! "
Loud on a sudden the cocks began to crow in the
    farm-yards,
Thinking the day had dawned ; and anon the low-
    ing of cattle
Came on the evening breeze, by the barking of
    dogs interrupted.
Then rose a sound of dread, such as startles the
    sleeping encampments

Far in the western prairies or forests that skirt the
 Nebraska,
When the wild horses affrighted sweep by with the
 speed of the whirlwind,
Or the loud bellowing herds of buffaloes rush to
 the river.
Such was the sound that arose on the night, as the
 herds and the horses
Broke through their folds and fences, and madly
 rushed o'er the meadows.

Overwhelmed with the sight, yet speechless, the
 priest and the maiden
Gazed on the scene of terror that reddened and
 widened before them ;
And as they turned at length to speak to their
 silent companion,
Lo ! from his seat he had fallen, and stretched
 abroad on the sea-shore
Motionless lay his form, from which the soul had
 departed.
Slowly the priest uplifted the lifeless head, and the
 maiden
Knelt at her father's side, and wailed aloud in her
 terror.
Then in a swoon she sank, and lay with her head
 on his bosom.
Through the long night she lay in deep, oblivious
 slumber ;

And when she woke from the trance, she beheld a
    multitude near her.
Faces of friends she beheld, that were mournfully
    gazing upon her,
Pallid, with tearful eyes, and looks of saddest com-
    passion.
Still the blaze of the burning village illumined the
    landscape,
Reddened the sky overhead, and gleamed on the
    faces around her,
And like the day of doom it seemed to her wavering
    senses.
Then a familiar voice she heard, as it said to the
    people, —
"Let us bury him here by the sea. When a hap-
    pier season
Brings us again to our homes from the unknown
    land of our exile,
Then shall his sacred dust be piously laid in the
    churchyard."
Such were the words of the priest. And there in
    haste by the sea-side,
Having the glare of the burning village for funeral
    torches,
But without bell or book, they buried the farmer of
    Grand-Pré.
And as the voice of the priest repeated the service
    of sorrow,
Lo! with a mournful sound, like the voice of a vast
    congregation,

Solemnly answered the sea, and mingled its roar
    with the dirges.

'T was the returning tide, that afar from the waste
    of the ocean,

With the first dawn of the day, came heaving and
    hurrying landward.

Then recommenced once more the stir and noise
    of embarking ;

And with the ebb of the tide the ships sailed out
    of the harbor,

Leaving behind them the dead on the shore, and
    the village in ruins.

PART THE SECOND

I.

MANY a weary year had passed since the
burning of Grand-Pré,
When on the falling tide the freighted vessels de-
parted,
Bearing a nation, with all its household gods, into
exile,·
Exile without an end, and without an example in
story.
Far asunder, on separate coasts, the Acadians
landed ;
Scattered were they, like flakes of snow, when the
wind from the northeast
Strikes aslant through the fogs that darken the
Banks of Newfoundland.
Friendless, homeless, hopeless, they wandered from
city to city,
From the cold lakes of the North to sultry Southern
savannas, —
From the bleak shores of the sea to the lands where
the Father of Waters

Seizes the hills in his hands, and drags them down
        to the ocean,
Deep in their sands to bury the scattered bones of
        the mammoth.
Friends they sought and homes; and many, de-
        spairing, heart-broken,
Asked of the earth but a grave, and no longer a
        friend nor a fireside.
Written their history stands on tablets of stone in
        the churchyards.
Long among them was seen a maiden who waited
        and wandered,
Lowly and meek in spirit, and patiently suffering
        all things.
Fair was she and young; but, alas! before her
        extended,
Dreary and vast and silent, the desert of life, with
        its pathway
Marked by the graves of those who had sorrowed
        and suffered before her,
Passions long extinguished, and hopes long dead
        and abandoned,
As the emigrant's way o'er the Western desert is
        marked by
Camp-fires long consumed, and bones that bleach
        in the sunshine.
Something there was in her life incomplete, imper-
        fect, unfinished;
As if a morning of June, with all its music and sun-
        shine,

Suddenly paused in the sky, and, fading, slowly
    descended
Into the east again, from whence it late had aris-
    en.
Sometimes she lingered in towns, till, urged by the
    fever within her,
Urged by a restless longing, the hunger and thirst
    of the spirit,
She would commence again her endless search and
    endeavor ;
Sometimes in churchyards strayed, and gazed on
    the crosses and tombstones,
Sat by some nameless grave, and thought that per-
    haps in its bosom
He was already at rest, and she longed to slumber
    beside him.
Sometimes a rumor, a hearsay, an inarticulate whis-
    per,
Came with its airy hand to point and beckon her
    forward.
Sometimes she spake with those who had seen her
    beloved and known him,
But it was long ago, in some far-off place or forgot-
    ten.
"Gabriel Lajeunesse!" they said; "O yes! we
    have seen him.
He was with Basil the blacksmith, and both have
    gone to the prairies ;
Coureurs-des-Bois are they, and famous hunters
    and trappers."

"Gabriel Lajeunesse!" said others; "O yes! we
    have seen him.

He is a Voyageur in the lowlands of Louisi-
    ana."

Then would they say, "Dear child! why dream
    and wait for him longer?

Are there not other youths as fair as Gabriel?
    others

Who have hearts as tender and true, and spirits as
    loyal?

Here is Baptiste Leblanc, the notary's son, who has
    loved thee

Many a tedious year; come, give him thy hand and
    be happy!

Thou art too fair to be left to braid St. Catherine's
    tresses."

Then would Evangeline answer, serenely but sad-
    ly, "I cannot!

Whither my heart has gone, there follows my hand,
    and not elsewhere.

For when the heart goes before, like a lamp, and
    illumines the pathway,

Many things are made clear, that else lie hidden in
    darkness."

Thereupon the priest, her friend and father-confes-
    sor,

Said, with a smile, "O daughter! thy God thus
    speaketh within thee!

Talk not of wasted affection, affection never was
    wasted;

If it enrich not the heart of another, its waters, returning

Back to their springs, like the rain, shall fill them full of refreshment ;

That which the fountain sends forth returns again to the fountain.

Patience ; accomplish thy labor ; accomplish thy work of affection !

Sorrow and silence are strong, and patient endurance is godlike.

Therefore accomplish thy labor of love, till the heart is made godlike,

Purified, strengthened, perfected, and rendered more worthy of heaven ! "

Cheered by the good man's words, Evangeline labored and waited.

Still in her heart she heard the funeral dirge of the ocean,

But with its sound there was mingled a voice that whispered, " Despair not ! "

Thus did that poor soul wander in want and cheerless discomfort,

Bleeding, barefooted, over the shards and thorns of existence.

Let me essay, O Muse ! to follow the wanderer's footsteps ; —

Not through each devious path, each changeful year of existence ;

But as a traveller follows a streamlet's course through the valley :

Far from its margin at times, and seeing the gleam
    of its water
Here and there, in some open space, and at inter-
    vals only;
Then drawing nearer its banks, through sylvan
    glooms that conceal it,
Though he behold it not, he can hear its continuous
    murmur;
Happy, at length, if he find the spot where it reach-
    es an outlet.

II.

It was the month of May. Far down the Beautiful
    River,
Past the Ohio shore and past the mouth of the Wa-
    bash,
Into the golden stream of the broad and swift Mis-
    sissippi,
Floated a cumbrous boat, that was rowed by Aca-
    dian boatmen.
It was a band of exiles: a raft, as it were, from the
    shipwrecked   .
Nation, scattered along the coast, now floating to-
    gether,
Bound by the bonds of a common belief and a
    common misfortune;

Men and women and children, who, guided by
    hope or by hearsay,
Sought for their kith and their kin among the few-
    acred farmers
On the Acadian coast, and the prairies of fair Ope-
    lousas.
With them Evangeline went, and her guide, the
    Father Felician.
Onward o'er sunken sands, through a wilderness
    sombre with forests,
Day after day they glided adown the turbulent
    river ;
Night after night, by their blazing fires, encamped
    on its borders.
Now through rushing chutes, among green islands,
    where plumelike
Cotton-trees nodded their shadowy crests, they
    swept with the current,
Then emerged into broad lagoons, where silvery
    sand-bars
Lay in the stream, and along the wimpling waves
    of their margin,
Shining with snow-white plumes, large flocks of
    pelicans waded.
Level the landscape grew, and along the shores of
    the river,
Shaded by china-trees, in the midst of luxuriant
    gardens,
Stood the houses of planters, with negro-cabins and
    dove-cots.

They were approaching the region where reigns
 perpetual summer,
Where through the Golden Coast, and groves of
 orange and citron,
Sweeps with majestic curve the river away to the
 eastward.
They, too, swerved from their course ; and, entering
 the Bayou of Plaquemine,
Soon were lost in a maze of sluggish and devious
 waters,
Which, like a network of steel, extended in every
 direction.
Over their heads the towering and tenebrous
 boughs of the cypress
Met in a dusky arch, and trailing mosses in mid
 air
Waved like banners that hang on the walls of ancient cathedrals.
Deathlike the silence seemed, and unbroken, save
 by the herons
Home to their roosts in the cedar-trees returning
 at sunset,
Or by the owl, as he greeted the moon with demo-
 niac laughter.
Lovely the moonlight was as it glanced and gleamed
 on the water,
Gleamed on the columns of cypress and cedar sustaining the arches,
Down through whose broken vaults it fell as
 through chinks in a ruin.

Dreamlike, and indistinct, and strange were all
    things around them ; ·

And o'er their spirits there came a feeling of won-
    der and sadness, —

Strange forebodings of ill, unseen and that cannot
    be compassed.

As, at the tramp of a horse's hoof on the turf of the
    prairies,

Far in advance are closed the leaves of the shrink-
    ing mimosa,

So, at the hoof-beats of fate, with sad forebodings
    of evil,

Shrinks and closes the heart, ere the stroke of
    doom has attained it.

But Evangeline's heart was sustained by a vision,
    that faintly

Floated before her eyes, and beckoned her on
    through the moonlight.

It was the thought of her brain that assumed the
    shape of a phantom.

Through those shadowy aisles had Gabriel wan-
    dered before her,

And every stroke of the oar now brought him
    nearer and nearer.

Then in his place, at the prow of the boat, rose
    one of the oarsmen,

And, as a signal sound, if others like them perad-
    venture

Sailed on those gloomy and midnight streams,
    blew a blast on his bugle.
Wild through the dark colonnades and corridors
    leafy the blast rang,
Breaking the seal of silence, and giving tongues to
    the forest.
Soundless above them the banners of moss just
    stirred to the music.
Multitudinous echoes awoke and died in the dis-
    tance,
Over the watery floor, and beneath the reverberant
    branches ;
But not a voice replied ; no answer came from the
    darkness ;
And, when the echoes had ceased, like a sense of
    pain was the silence.
Then Evangeline slept ; but the boatmen rowed
    through the midnight,
Silent at times, then singing familiar Canadian
    boat-songs,
Such as they sang of old on their own Acadian
    rivers,
While through the night were heard the mysterious
    sounds of the desert,
Far off, — indistinct, — as of wave or wind in the
    forest,
Mixed with the whoop of the crane and the roar of
    the grim alligator.

Thus ere another noon they emerged from the
    shades ; and before them
Lay, in the golden sun, the lakes of the Atcha-
    falaya.
Water-lilies in myriads rocked on the slight undu-
    lations
Made by the passing oars, and, resplendent in
    beauty, the lotus
Lifted her golden crown above the heads of the
    boatmen.
Faint was the air with the odorous breath of mag-
    nolia blossoms,
And with the heat of noon ; and numberless syl-
    van islands,
Fragrant and thickly embowered with blossoming
    hedges of roses,
Near to whose shores they glided along, invited to
    slumber.
Soon by the fairest of these their weary oars were
    suspended.
Under the boughs of Wachita willows, that grew
    by the margin,
Safely their boat was moored ; and scattered about
    on the greensward,
Tired with their midnight toil, the weary travellers
    slumbered.
Over them vast and high extended the cope of a
    cedar.
Swinging from its great arms, the trumpet-flower
    and the grape-vine

Hung their ladder of ropes aloft like the ladder of
    Jacob,
On whose pendulous stairs the angels ascending,
    descending,
Were the swift humming-birds, that flitted from
    blossom to blossom.
Such was the vision Evangeline saw as she slum-
    bered beneath it.
Filled was her heart with love, and the dawn of an
    opening heaven
Lighted her soul in sleep with the glory of regions
    celestial.

   Nearer and ever nearer, among the numberless
    islands,
Darted a light, swift boat, that sped away o'er the
    water,
Urged on its course by the sinewy arms of hunters
    and trappers.
Northward its prow was turned, to the land of the
    bison and beaver.
At the helm sat a youth, with countenance thought-
    ful and careworn.
Dark and neglected locks overshadowed his brow,
    and a sadness
Somewhat beyond his years on his face was legibly
    written.
Gabriel was it, who, weary with waiting, unhappy
    and restless,

Sought in the Western wilds oblivion of self and of
    sorrow.

Swiftly they glided along, close under the lee of the
    island,

But by the opposite bank, and behind a screen of
    palmettos,

So that they saw not the boat, where it lay con-
    cealed in the willows,

All undisturbed by the dash of their oars, and un-
    seen, were the sleepers,

Angel of God was there none to awaken the slum-
    bering maiden.

Swiftly they glided away, like the shade of a cloud
    on the prairie.

After the sound of their oars on the tholes had died
    in the distance,

As from a magic trance the sleepers awoke, and
    the maiden

Said with a sigh to the friendly priest, "O Father
    Felician!

Something says in my heart that near me Gabriel
    wanders.

Is it a foolish dream, an idle and vague supersti-
    tion?

Or has an angel passed, and revealed the truth to
    my spirit?"

Then, with a blush, she added, "Alas for my cred-
    ulous fancy!

Unto ears like thine such words as these have no
    meaning."

But made answer the reverend man, and he smiled
    as he answered, —

"Daughter, thy words are not idle; nor are they to
    me without meaning.

Feeling is deep and still; and the word that floats
    on the surface

Is as the tossing buoy, that betrays where the an-
    chor is hidden.

Therefore trust to thy heart, and to what the world
    calls illusions.

Gabriel truly is near thee; for not far away to the
    southward,

On the banks of the Têche, are the towns of St.
    Maur and St. Martin.

There the long-wandering bride shall be given
    again to her bridegroom,

There the long-absent pastor regain his flock and
    his sheepfold.

Beautiful is the land, with its prairies and forests of
    fruit-trees;

Under the feet a garden of flowers, and the bluest
    of heavens

Bending above, and resting its dome on the walls of
    the forest.

They who dwell there have named it the Eden of
    Louisiana."

With these words of cheer they arose and contin-
    ued their journey.

Softly the evening came. The sun from the western
    horizon
Like a magician extended his golden wand o'er the
    landscape ;
Twinkling vapors arose ; and sky and water and
    forest
Seemed all on fire at the touch, and melted and
    mingled together.
Hanging between two skies, a cloud with edges of
    silver,
Floated the boat, with its dripping oars, on the mo-
    tionless water.
Filled was Evangeline's heart with inexpressible
    sweetness.
Touched by the magic spell, the sacred fountains
    of feeling
Glowed with the light of love, as the skies and wa-
    ters around her.
Then from a neighboring thicket the mocking-bird,
    wildest of singers,
Swinging aloft on a willow spray that hung o'er the
    water,
Shook from his little throat such floods of delirious
    music,
That the whole air and the woods and the waves
    seemed silent to listen.
Plaintive at first were the tones and sad ; then
    soaring to madness
Seemed they to follow or guide the revel of frenzied
    Bacchantes.

Single notes were then heard, in sorrowful, low
      lamentation ;
Till, having gathered them all, he flung them abroad
      in derision,
As when, after a storm, a gust of wind through the
      tree-tops
Shakes down the rattling rain in a crystal shower
      on the branches.
With such a prelude as this, and hearts that
      throbbed with emotion,
Slowly they entered the Têche, where it flows
      through the green Opelousas,
And, through the amber air, above the crest of the
      woodland,
Saw the column of smoke that arose from a neigh-
      boring dwelling ; —
Sounds of a horn they heard, and the distant lowing
      of cattle.

III.

NEAR to the bank of the river, o'ershadowed by
      oaks, from whose branches
Garlands of Spanish moss and of mystic mistletoe
      flaunted,
Such as the Druids cut down with golden hatchets
      at Yule-tide,

Stood, secluded and still, the house of the herdsman. A garden

Girded it round about with a belt of luxuriant blossoms,

Filling the air with fragrance. The house itself was
of timbers

Hewn from the cypress-tree, and carefully fitted
together.

Large and low was the roof; and on slender columns supported,

Rose-wreathed, vine-encircled, a broad and spacious
veranda,

Haunt of the humming-bird and the bee, extended
around it.

At each end of the house, amid the flowers of the
garden,

Stationed the dove-cots were, as love's perpetual
symbol,

Scenes of endless wooing, and endless contentions
of rivals.

Silence reigned o'er the place. The line of shadow
and sunshine

Ran near the tops of the trees; but the house itself
was in shadow,

And from its chimney-top, ascending and slowly
expanding

Into the evening air, a thin blue column of smoke
rose.

In the rear of the house, from the garden gate, ran
a pathway

Through the great groves of oak to the skirts of the
    limitless prairie,
Into whose sea of flowers the sun was slowly de-
    scending.
Full in his track of light, like ships with shadowy
    canvas
Hanging loose from their spars in a motionless calm
    in the tropics,
Stood a cluster of trees, with tangled cordage of
    grape-vines.

  Just where the woodlands met the flowery surf of
    the prairie,
Mounted upon his horse, with Spanish saddle and
    stirrups,
Sat a herdsman, arrayed in gaiters and doublet of
    deerskin.
Broad and brown was the face that from under the
    Spanish sombrero
Gazed on the peaceful scene, with the lordly look
    of its master.
Round about him were numberless herds of kine,
    that were grazing
Quietly in the meadows, and breathing the vapory
    freshness
That uprose from the river, and spread itself over
    the landscape.
Slowly lifting the horn that hung at his side, and
    expanding

Fully his broad, deep chest, he blew a blast, that
    resounded
Wildly and sweet and far, through the still damp
    air of the evening.
Suddenly out of the grass the long white horns of
    the cattle
Rose like flakes of foam on the adverse currents of
    ocean.
Silent a moment they gazed, then bellowing rushed
    o'er the prairie,
And the whole mass became a cloud, a shade in
    the distance.
Then, as the herdsman turned to the house, through
    the gate of the garden
Saw he the forms of the priest and the maiden
    advancing to meet him.
Suddenly down from his horse he sprang in amaze-
    ment, and forward
Rushed with extended arms and exclamations of
    wonder;
When they beheld his face, they recognized Basil
    the blacksmith.
Hearty his welcome was, as he led his guests to the
    garden.
There in an arbor of roses with endless question and
    answer
Gave they vent to their hearts, and renewed their
    friendly embraces,
Laughing and weeping by turns, or sitting silent
    and thoughtful.

7 *

Thoughtful, for Gabriel came not; and now dark
    doubts and misgivings
Stole o'er the maiden's heart; and Basil, somewhat
    embarrassed,
Broke the silence and said, "If you came by the
    Atchafalaya,
How have you nowhere encountered my Gabriel's
    boat on the bayous?"
Over Evangeline's face at the words of Basil a
    shade passed.
Tears came into her eyes, and she said, with a
    tremulous accent,
"Gone? is Gabriel gone?" and, concealing her
    face on his shoulder,
All her o'erburdened heart gave way, and she wept
    and lamented.
Then the good Basil said, — and his voice grew
    blithe as he said it, —
"Be of good cheer, my child; it is only to-day he
    departed.
Foolish boy! he has left me alone with my herds
    and my horses.
Moody and restless grown, and tried and troubled,
    his spirit
Could no longer endure the calm of this quiet exist-
    ence.
Thinking ever of thee, uncertain and sorrowful
    ever,
Ever silent, or speaking only of thee and his troub-
    les,

He at length had become so tedious to men and to
    maidens,
Tedious even to me, that at length I bethought me,
    and sent him
Unto the town of Adayes to trade for mules with
    the Spaniards.
Thence he will follow the Indian trails to the Ozark
    Mountains,
Hunting for furs in the forests, on rivers trapping
    the beaver.
Therefore be of good cheer; we will follow the
    fugitive lover;
He is not far on his way, and the Fates and the
    streams are against him.
Up and away to-morrow, and through the red dew
    of the morning
We will follow him fast, and bring him back to his
    prison."

Then glad voices were heard, and up from the
    banks of the river,
Borne aloft on his comrades' arms, came Michael
    the fiddler.
Long under Basil's roof had he lived like a god on
    Olympus,
Having no other care than dispensing music to
    mortals.
Far renowned was he for his silver locks and his
    fiddle.

"Long live Michael," they cried, "our brave Aca-
    dian minstrel !"
As they bore him aloft in triumphal procession ;
    and straightway
Father Felician advanced with Evangeline, greeting
    the old man
Kindly and oft, and recalling the past, while Basil,
    enraptured,
Hailed with hilarious joy his old companions and
    gossips,
Laughing loud and long, and embracing mothers
    and daughters.
Much they marvelled to see the wealth of the ci-
    devant blacksmith,
All his domains and his herds, and his patriarchal
    demeanor ;
Much they marvelled to hear his tales of the soil
    and the climate,
And of the prairies, whose numberless herds were
    his who would take them ;
Each one thought in his heart, that he, too, would
    go and do likewise.
Thus they ascended the steps, and, crossing the
    breezy veranda,
Entered the hall of the house, where already the
    supper of Basil
Waited his late return ; and they rested and feasted
    together.

Over the joyous feast the sudden darkness
    descended.

All was silent without, and, illuming the landscape
    with silver,

Fair rose the dewy moon and the myriad stars;
    but within doors,

Brighter than these, shone the faces of friends in
    the glimmering lamplight.

Then from his station aloft, at the head of the table,
    the herdsman

Poured forth his heart and his wine together in
    endless profusion.

Lighting his pipe, that was filled with sweet Natchi-
    toches tobacco,

Thus he spake to his guests, who listened, and
    smiled as they listened: —

"Welcome once more, my friends, who long have
    been friendless and homeless,

Welcome once more to a home, that is better per-
    chance than the old one!

Here no hungry winter congeals our blood like the
    rivers;

Here no stony ground provokes the wrath of the
    farmer.

Smoothly the ploughshare runs through the soil, as
    a keel through the water.

All the year round the orange-groves are in blos-
    som; and grass grows

More in a single night than a whole Canadian sum-
    mer.

Here, too, numberless herds run wild and unclaimed
    in the prairies ;
Here, too, lands may be had for the asking, and
    forests of timber
With a few blows of the axe are hewn and framed
    into houses.
After your houses are built, and your fields are yel-
    low with harvests,
No King George of England shall drive you away
    from your homesteads,
Burning your dwellings and barns, and stealing
    your farms and your cattle."
Speaking these words, he blew a wrathful cloud
    from his nostrils,
While his huge, brown hand came thundering
    down on the table,
So that the guests all started ; and Father Felician,
    astounded,
Suddenly paused, with a pinch of snuff half-way to
    his nostrils.
But the brave Basil resumed, and his words were
    milder and gayer :—
"Only beware of the fever, my friends, beware of
    the fever !
For it is not like that of our cold Acadian
    climate,
Cured by wearing a spider hung round one's neck
    in a nutshell !"
Then there were voices heard at the door, and foot-
    steps approaching

Sounded upon the stairs and the floor of the breezy
    veranda.
It was the neighboring Creoles and small Acadian
    planters,
Who had been summoned all to the house of Basil
    the Herdsman.
Merry the meeting was of ancient comrades and
    neighbors :
Friend clasped friend in his arms ; and they who
    before were as strangers,
Meeting in exile, became straightway as friends to
    each other,
Drawn by the gentle bond of a common country
    together.
But in the neighboring hall a strain of music, pro-
    ceeding
From the accordant strings of Michael's melodious
    fiddle,
Broke up all further speech. Away, like children
    delighted,
All things forgotten beside, they gave themselves to
    the maddening
Whirl of the dizzy dance, as it swept and swayed to
    the music,
Dreamlike, with beaming eyes and the rush of flut-
    tering garments.

    Meanwhile, apart, at the head of the hall, the
    priest and the herdsman

Sat, conversing together of past and present and
    future ;

While Evangeline stood like one entranced, for
    within her

Olden memories rose, and loud in the midst of the
    music

Heard she the sound of the sea, and an irrepressi-
    ble sadness

Came o'er her heart, and unseen she stole forth
    into the garden.

Beautiful was the night.   Behind the black wall of
    the forest,

Tipping its summit with silver, arose the moon.
    On the river

Fell here and there through the branches a tremu-
    lous gleam of the moonlight,   .

Like the sweet thoughts of love on a darkened and
    devious spirit.

Nearer and round about her, the manifold flowers
    of the garden

Poured out their souls in odors, that were their
    prayers and confessions

Unto the night, as it went its way, like a silent Car-
    thusian.

Fuller of fragrance than they, and as heavy with
    shadows and night-dews,

Hung the heart of the maiden.   The calm and the
    magical moonlight

Seemed to inundate her soul with indefinable long-
    ings,

As, through the garden gate, and beneath the shade
    of the oak-trees,
Passed she along the path to the edge of the meas-
    ureless prairie.
Silent it lay, with a silvery haze upon it, and fire-
    flies
Gleaming and floating away in mingled and infinite
    numbers.
Over her head the stars, the thoughts of God in the
    heavens,
Shone on the eyes of man, who had ceased to mar-
    vel and worship,
Save when a blazing comet was seen on the walls
    of that temple,
As if a hand had appeared and written upon them,
    " Upharsin."
And the soul of the maiden, between the stars and
    the fire-flies,
Wandered alone, and she cried, "O Gabriel! O
    my beloved!
Art thou so near unto me, and yet I cannot behold
    thee?
Art thou so near unto me, and yet thy voice does
    not reach me?
Ah! how often thy feet have trod this path to the
    prairie!
Ah! how often thine eyes have looked on the
    woodlands around me!
Ah! how often beneath this oak, returning from
    labor,

Thou hast lain down to rest, and to dream of me in
    thy slumbers.
When shall these eyes behold, these arms be folded
    about thee?"
Loud and sudden and near the note of a whippoor-
    will sounded
Like a flute in the woods; and anon, through the
    neighboring thickets,
Farther and farther away it floated and dropped
    into silence.
"Patience!" whispered the oaks from oracular cav-
    erns of darkness;
And, from the moonlit meadow, a sigh responded,
    "To-morrow!"

Bright rose the sun next day; and all the flowers
    of the garden
Bathed his shining feet with their tears, and anoint-
    ed his tresses
With the delicious balm that they bore in their
    vases of crystal.
"Farewell!" said the priest, as he stood at the
    shadowy threshold;
"See that you bring us the Prodigal Son from his
    fasting and famine,
And, too, the Foolish Virgin, who slept when the
    bridegroom was coming."
"Farewell!" answered the maiden, and, smiling,
    with Basil descended

Down to the river's brink, where the boatmen al-
    ready were waiting.
Thus beginning their journey with morning, and
    sunshine, and gladness,
Swiftly they followed the flight of him who was
    speeding before them,
Blown by the blast of fate like a dead leaf over the
    desert.
Not that day, nor the next, nor yet the day that
    succeeded,
Found they trace of his course, in lake or forest or
    river,
Nor, after many days, had they found him; but
    vague and uncertain
Rumors alone were their guides through a wild and
    desolate country;
Till, at the little inn of the Spanish town of
    Adayes,
Weary and worn, they alighted, and learned from
    the garrulous landlord,
That on the day before, with horses and guides and
    companions,
Gabriel left the village, and took the road of the
    prairies.

IV.

FAR in the West there lies a desert land, where the
   mountains
Lift, through perpetual snows, their lofty and lumi-
   nous summits.
Down from their jagged, deep ravines, where the
   gorge, like a gateway,
Opens a passage rude to the wheels of the emi-
   grant's wagon,
Westward the Oregon flows and the Walleway and
   Owyhee.
Eastward, with devious course, among the Wind-
   river Mountains,
Through the Sweet-water Valley precipitate leaps
   the Nebraska ;
And to the south, from Fontaine-qui-bout and the
   Spanish sierras,
Fretted with sands and rocks, and swept by the
   wind of the desert,
Numberless torrents, with ceaseless sound, descend
   to the ocean,
Like the great chords of a harp, in loud and solemn
   vibrations.
Spreading between these streams are the wondrous,
   beautiful prairies,
Billowy bays of grass ever rolling in shadow and
   sunshine,

Bright with luxuriant clusters of roses and purple
    amorphas.
Over them wandered the buffalo herds, and the elk
    and the roebuck ;
Over them wandered the wolves, and herds of rider-
    less horses ;
Fires that blast and blight, and winds that are
    weary with travel ;
Over them wander the scattered tribes of Ishmael's
    children,
Staining the desert with blood ; and above their
    terrible war-trails
Circles and sails aloft, on pinions majestic, the vul-
    ture,
Like the implacable soul of a chieftain slaughtered
    in battle,
By invisible stairs ascending and scaling the heav-
    ens.
Here and there rise smokes from the camps of
    these savage marauders ;
Here and there rise groves from the margins of
    swift-running rivers ;
And the grim, taciturn bear, the anchorite monk
    of the desert,
Climbs down their dark ravines to dig for roots by
    the brook-side,
And over all is the sky, the clear and crystalline
    heaven,
Like the protecting hand of God inverted above
    them.

Into this wonderful land, at the base of the
    Ozark Mountains,
Gabriel far had entered, with hunters and trappers
    behind him.
Day after day, with their Indian guides, the maiden -
    and Basil
Followed his flying steps, and thought each day to
    o'ertake him.
Sometimes they saw, or thought they saw, the
    smoke of his camp-fire
Rise in the morning air from the distant plain;
    but at nightfall,
When they had reached the place, they found only
    embers and ashes.
And, though their hearts were sad at times and
    their bodies were weary,
Hope still guided them on, as the magic Fata
    Morgana
Showed them her lakes of light, that retreated and
    vanished before them.

Once, as they sat by their evening fire, there si-
    lently entered
Into the little camp an Indian woman, whose fea-
    tures
Wore deep traces of sorrow, and patience as great
    as her sorrow.
She was a Shawnee woman returning home to her
    people,

From the far-off hunting-grounds of the cruel Ca-
    manches,
Where her Canadian husband, a Coureur-des-Bois,
    had been murdered.
Touched were their hearts at her story, and warm-
    est and friendliest welcome
Gave they, with words of cheer, and she sat and
    feasted among them
On the buffalo-meat and the venison cooked on the
    embers.
But when their meal was done, and Basil and all
    his companions,
Worn with the long day's march and the chase of
    the deer and the bison,
Stretched themselves on the ground, and slept
    where the quivering fire-light
Flashed on their swarthy cheeks, and their forms
    wrapped up in their blankets,
Then at the door of Evangeline's tent she sat and
    repeated
Slowly, with soft, low voice, and the charm of her
    Indian accent,
All the tale of her love, with its pleasures, and
    pains, and reverses.
Much Evangeline wept at the tale, and to know
    that another
Hapless heart like her own had loved and had
    been disappointed.
Moved to the depths of her soul by pity and wom-
    an's compassion,

Yet in her sorrow pleased that one who had suf-
        fered was near her,
She in turn related her love and all its disas-
        ters.
Mute with wonder the Shawnee sat, and when she
        had ended
Still was mute; but at length, as if a mysterious
        horror
Passed through her brain, she spake, and repeated
        the tale of the Mowis;
Mowis, the bridegroom of snow, who won and
        wedded a maiden,
But, when the morning came, arose and passed
        from the wigwam,
Fading and melting away and dissolving into the
        sunshine,
Till she beheld him no more, though she followed
        far into the forest.
Then, in those sweet, low tones, that seemed like
        a weird incantation,
Told she the tale of the fair Lilinau, who was
        wooed by a phantom,
That, through the pines o'er her father's lodge, in
        the hush of the twilight,
Breathed like the evening wind, and whispered
        love to the maiden,
Till she followed his green and waving plume
        through the forest,
And never more returned, nor was seen again by
        her people.

Silent with wonder and strange surprise, Evangeline listened
To the soft flow of her magical words, till the region around her
Seemed like enchanted ground, and her swarthy
guest the enchantress.
Slowly over the tops of the Ozark Mountains the
moon rose,
Lighting the little tent, and with a mysterious
splendor
Touching the sombre leaves, and embracing and
filling the woodland.
With a delicious sound the brook rushed by, and
the branches
Swayed and sighed overhead in scarcely audible
whispers.
Filled with the thoughts of love was Evangeline's
heart, but a secret,
Subtile sense crept in of pain and indefinite terror,
As the cold, poisonous snake creeps into the nest
of the swallow.
It was no earthly fear. A breath from the region
of spirits
Seemed to float in the air of night; and she felt
for a moment
That, like the Indian maid, she, too, was pursuing
a phantom.
With this thought she slept, and the fear and the
phantom had vanished.

Early upon the morrow the march was resumed ;
and the Shawnee

Said, as they journeyed along, " On the western
slope of these mountains

Dwells in his little village the Black Robe chief of
the Mission.

Much he teaches the people, and tells them of
Mary and Jesus ;

Loud laugh their hearts with joy, and weep with
pain, as they hear him."

Then, with a sudden and secret emotion, Evangeline answered,

" Let us go to the Mission, for there good tidings
await us ! "

Thither they turned their steeds ; and behind a
spur of the mountains,

Just as the sun went down, they heard a murmur of
voices,

And in a meadow green and broad, by the bank of
a river,

Saw the tents of the Christians, the tents of the
Jesuit Mission.

Under a towering oak, that stood in the midst of
the village,

Knelt the Black Robe chief with his children.   A
crucifix fastened

High on the trunk of the tree, and overshadowed
by grape-vines,

Looked with its agonized face on the multitude
kneeling beneath it.

This was their rural chapel. Aloft, through the
    intricate arches
Of its aerial roof, arose the chant of their ves-
    pers,
Mingling its notes with the soft susurrus and sighs
    of the branches.
Silent, with heads uncovered, the travellers, nearer
    approaching,
Knelt on the swarded floor, and joined in the even-
    ing devotions.
But when the service was done, and the benedic-
    tion had fallen
Forth from the hands of the priest, like seed from
    the hands of the sower,
Slowly the reverend man advanced to the strangers,
    and bade them
Welcome ; and when they replied, he smiled with
    benignant expression,
Hearing the homelike sounds of his mother-tongue
    in the forest,
And, with words of kindness, conducted them into
    his wigwam.
There upon mats and skins they reposed, and on
    cakes of the maize-ear
Feasted, and slaked their thirst from the water-
    gourd of the teacher.
Soon was their story told ; and the priest with so-
    lemnity answered :—
" Not six suns have risen and set since Gabriel,
    seated

On this mat by my side, where now the maiden
    reposes,
Told me this same sad tale; then arose and con-
    tinued his journey!"
Soft was the voice of the priest, and he spake with
    an accent of kindness;
But on Evangeline's heart fell his words as in win-
    ter the snow-flakes
Fall into some lone nest from which the birds have
    departed.
"Far to the north he has gone," continued the
    priest; "but in autumn,
When the chase is done, will return again to the
    Mission."
Then Evangeline said, and her voice was meek
    and submissive,
"Let me remain with thee, for my soul is sad and
    afflicted."
So seemed it wise and well unto all; and betimes
    on the morrow,
Mounting his Mexican steed, with his Indian guides
    and companions,
Homeward Basil returned, and Evangeline stayed
    at the Mission.

Slowly, slowly, slowly the days succeeded each
    other, —
Days and weeks and months; and the fields of
    maize that were springing

Green from the ground when a stranger she came,
  now waving above her,
Lifted their slender shafts, with leaves interlacing,
  and forming
Cloisters for mendicant crows and granaries pillaged by squirrels.
Then in the golden weather the maize was husked,
  and the maidens
Blushed at each blood-red ear, for that betokened
  a lover,
But at the crooked laughed, and called it a thief in
  the corn-field.
Even the blood-red ear to Evangeline brought not
  her lover.
" Patience ! " the priest would say ; " have faith,
  and thy prayer will be answered !
Look at this simple plant that lifts its head from
  the meadow,
See how its leaves are turned to the north, as true
  as the magnet ;
This is the compass-flower, that the finger of God
  has planted
Here in the houseless wild, to direct the traveller's
  journey
Over the sea-like, pathless, limitless waste of the
  desert.
Such in the soul of man is faith. The blossoms of
  passion,
Gay and luxuriant flowers, are brighter and fuller
  of fragrance,

But they beguile us, and lead us astray, and their
    odor is deadly.
Only this humble plant can guide us here, and
    hereafter
Crown us with asphodel flowers, that are wet with
    the dews of nepenthe."

So came the autumn, and passed, and the win-
    ter, — yet Gabriel came not ;
Blossomed the opening spring, and the notes of the
    robin and bluebird
Sounded sweet upon wold and in wood, yet Gabriel
    came not.
But on the breath of the summer winds a rumor was
    wafted
Sweeter than song of bird, or hue or odor of blos-
    som.
Far to the north and east, it said, in the Michigan
    forests,
Gabriel had his lodge by the banks of the Saginaw
    river.
And, with returning guides, that sought the lakes
    of St. Lawrence,
Saying a sad farewell, Evangeline went from the
    Mission.
When over weary ways, by long and perilous
    marches,
She had attained at length the depths of the Michi-
    gan forests,

Found she the hunter's lodge deserted and fallen to
    ruin !

Thus did the long sad years glide on, and in
    seasons and places
Divers and distant far was seen the wandering
    maiden ; —
Now in the Tents of Grace of the meek Moravian
    Missions,
Now in the noisy camps and the battle-fields of the
    army,
Now in secluded hamlets, in towns and populous
    cities.
Like a phantom she came, and passed away unre-
    membered.
Fair was she and young, when in hope began the
    long journey ;
Faded was she and old, when in disappointment it
    ended.
Each succeeding year stole something away from
    her beauty,
Leaving behind it, broader and deeper, the gloom
    and the shadow.
Then there appeared and spread faint streaks of
    gray o'er her forehead,
Dawn of another life, that broke o'er her earthly
    horizon,
As in the eastern sky the first faint streaks of the
    morning.

V.

In that delightful land which is washed by the
    Delaware's waters,
Guarding in sylvan shades the name of Penn the
    apostle,
Stands on the banks of its beautiful stream the
    city he founded.
There all the air is balm, and the peach is the
    emblem of beauty,
And the streets still re-echo the names of the trees
    of the forest,
As if they fain would appease the Dryads whose
    haunts they molested.
There from the troubled sea had Evangeline landed,
    an exile,
Finding among the children of Penn a home and a
    country.
There old René Leblanc had died; and when he
    departed,
Saw at his side only one of all his hundred de-
    scendants.
Something at least there was in the friendly streets
    of the city,
Something that spake to her heart, and made her
    no longer a stranger;
And her ear was pleased with the Thee and Thou
    of the Quakers,

For it recalled the past, the old Acadian coun-
    try,
Where all men were equal, and all were brothers
    and sisters.
So, when the fruitless search, the disappointed en-
    deavor,
Ended, to recommence no more upon earth, un-
    complaining,
Thither, as leaves to the light, were turned her
    thoughts and her footsteps.
As from a mountain's top the rainy mists of the
    morning
Roll away, and afar we behold the landscape
    below us,
Sun-illumined, with shining rivers and cities and
    hamlets,
So fell the mists from her mind, and she saw the
    world far below her,
Dark no longer, but all illumined with love ; and
    the pathway
Which she had climbed so far, lying smooth and
    fair in the distance.
Gabriel was not forgotten. Within her heart was
    his image,
Clothed in the beauty of love and youth, as last
    she beheld him,
Only more beautiful made by his deathlike silence
    and absence.
Into her thoughts of him time entered not, for it
    was not.

Over him years had no power ; he was not changed,
     but transfigured ;
He had become to her heart as one who is dead,
     and not absent ;
Patience and abnegation of self, and devotion to
     others,
This was the lesson a life of trial and sorrow had
     taught her.
So was her love diffused, but, like to some odorous
     spices,
Suffered no waste nor loss, though filling the air
     with aroma.
Other hope had she none, nor wish in life, but to
     follow
Meekly, with reverent steps, the sacred feet of her
     Saviour.
Thus many years she lived as a Sister of Mercy ;
     frequenting
Lonely and wretched roofs in the crowded lanes
     of the city,
Where distress and want concealed themselves
     from the sunlight,
Where disease and sorrow in garrets languished
     neglected.
Night after night, when the world was asleep, as
     the watchman repeated
Loud, through the gusty streets, that all was well
     in the city,
High at some lonely window he saw the light of
     her taper.

Day after day, in the gray of the dawn, as slow
    through the suburbs
Plodded the German farmer, with flowers and fruits
    for the market,
Met he that meek, pale face, returning home from
    its watchings.

Then it came to pass that a pestilence fell on the
    city,
Presaged by wondrous signs, and mostly by flocks
    of wild pigeons,
Darkening the sun in their flight, with naught in
    their craws but an acorn.
And, as the tides of the sea arise in the month of
    September,
Flooding some silver stream, till it spreads to a
    lake in the meadow,
So death flooded life, and, o'erflowing its natural
    margin,
Spread to a brackish lake, the silver stream of
    existence.
Wealth had no power to bribe, nor beauty to charm,
    the oppressor ;
But all perished alike beneath the scourge of his
    anger ; —
Only, alas ! the poor, who had neither friends nor
    attendants,
Crept away to die in the almshouse, home of the
    homeless.

Then in the suburbs it stood, in the midst of mead-
  ows and woodlands ;—
Now the city surrounds it; but still, with its gate-
  way and wicket
Meek, in the midst of splendor, its humble walls
  seem to echo
Softly the words of the Lord :—"The poor ye
  always have with you."
Thither, by night and by day, came the Sister of
  Mercy. The dying
Looked up into her face, and thought, indeed, to
  behold there
Gleams of celestial light encircle her forehead with
  splendor,
Such as the artist paints o'er the brows of saints
  and apostles,
Or such as hangs by night o'er a city seen at a
  distance.
Unto their eyes it seemed the lamps of the city
  celestial,
Into whose shining gates erelong their spirits would
  enter.

  Thus, on a Sabbath morn, through the streets,
    deserted and silent,
Wending her quiet way, she entered the door of
  the almshouse.
Sweet on the summer air was the odor of flowers
    in the garden ;

And she paused on her way to gather the fairest
    among them,
That the dying once more might rejoice in their
    fragrance and beauty.
Then, as she mounted the stairs to the corridors,
    cooled by the east wind,
Distant and soft on her ear fell the chimes from
    the belfry of Christ Church,
While, intermingled with these, across the meadows
    were wafted
Sounds of psalms, that were sung by the Swedes in
    their church at Wicaco.
Soft as descending wings fell the calm of the hour
    on her spirit ;
Something within her said, " At length thy trials are
    ended " ;
And, with light in her looks, she entered the cham-
    bers of sickness.
Noiselessly moved about the assiduous, careful at-
    tendants,
Moistening the feverish lip, and the aching brow,
    and in silence
Closing the sightless eyes of the dead, and conceal-
    ing their faces,
Where on their pallets they lay, like drifts of snow
    by the roadside.
Many a languid head, upraised as Evangeline
    entered,
Turned on its pillow of pain to gaze while she
    passed, for her presence

Fell on their hearts like a ray of the sun on the
walls of a prison.
And, as she looked around, she saw how Death,
the consoler,
Laying his hand upon many a heart, had healed it
forever.
Many familiar forms had disappeared in the night-
time ;
Vacant their places were, or filled already by strangers.

Suddenly, as if arrested by fear or a feeling of
wonder,
Still she stood, with her colorless lips apart, while
a shudder
Ran through her frame, and, forgotten, the flow-
erets dropped from her fingers,
And from her eyes and cheeks the light and bloom
of the morning.
Then there escaped from her lips a cry of such terrible anguish,
That the dying heard it, and started up from their
pillows.
On the pallet before her was stretched the form of
an old man.
Long, and thin, and gray were the locks that shaded his temples ;
But, as he lay in the morning light, his face for a
moment

Seemed to assume once more the forms of its ear-
lier manhood ;

So are wont to be changed the faces of those who
are dying.

Hot and red on his lips still burned the flush of the
fever,

As if life, like the Hebrew, with blood had be-
sprinkled its portals,

That the Angel of Death might see the sign, and
pass over.

Motionless, senseless, dying, he lay, and his spirit
exhausted

Seemed to be sinking down through infinite depths
in the darkness,

Darkness of slumber and death, forever sinking
and sinking.

Then through those realms of shade, in multiplied
reverberations,

Heard he that cry of pain, and through the hush
that succeeded

Whispered a gentle voice, in accents tender and
saint-like,

"Gabriel! O my beloved!" and died away into
silence.

Then he beheld, in a dream, once more the home
of his childhood ;

Green Acadian meadows, with sylvan rivers among
them,

Village, and mountain, and woodlands ; and, walking under their shadow,

As in the days of her youth, Evangeline rose in his
vision.
Tears came into his eyes; and as slowly he lifted
his eyelids,
Vanished the vision away, but Evangeline knelt by
his bedside.
Vainly he strove to whisper her name, for the accents unuttered
Died on his lips, and their motion revealed what
his tongue would have spoken.
Vainly he strove to rise; and Evangeline, kneeling
beside him,
Kissed his dying lips, and laid his head on her
bosom.
Sweet was the light of his eyes; but it suddenly
sank into darkness,
As when a lamp is blown out by a gust of wind at
a casement.

All was ended now, the hope, and the fear, and
the sorrow,
All the aching of heart, the restless, unsatisfied
longing,
All the dull, deep pain, and constant anguish of
patience!
And, as she pressed once more the lifeless head to
her bosom,
Meekly she bowed her own, and murmured, "Father, I thank thee!"

STILL stands the forest primeval; but far away
    from its shadow,
Side by side, in their nameless graves, the lovers
    are sleeping.
Under the humble walls of the little Catholic
    churchyard,
In the heart of the city, they lie, unknown and
    unnoticed.
Daily the tides of life go ebbing and flowing beside
    them,
Thousands of throbbing hearts, where theirs are at
    rest and forever,
Thousands of aching brains, where theirs no longer
    are busy,
Thousands of toiling hands, where theirs have
    ceased from their labors,
Thousands of weary feet, where theirs have com-
    pleted their journey!

    Still stands the forest primeval; but under the
    shade of its branches
Dwells another race, with other customs and lan-
    guage.
Only along the shore of the mournful and misty
    Atlantic
Linger a few Acadian peasants, whose fathers from
    exile

Wandered back to their native land to die in its
    bosom.

In the fisherman's cot the wheel and the loom are
    still busy;

Maidens still wear their Norman caps and their kir-
    tles of homespun,

And by the evening fire repeat Evangeline's
    story,

While from its rocky caverns the deep-voiced,
    neighboring ocean

Speaks, and in accents disconsolate answers the
    wail of the forest.

THE SEASIDE

AND THE FIRESIDE.

1849

DEDICATION.

As one who, walking in the twilight gloom,
  Hears round about him voices as it darkens,
And seeing not the forms from which they come,
  Pauses from time to time, and turns and hark-
    ens;

So walking here in twilight, O my friends!
  I hear your voices, softened by the distance,
And pause, and turn to listen, as each sends
  His words of friendship, comfort, and assistance.

If any thought of mine, or sung or told,
  Has ever given delight or consolation,
Ye have repaid me back a thousand-fold,
  By every friendly sign and salutation.

Thanks for the sympathies that ye have shown!
  Thanks for each kindly word, each silent token,
That teaches me, when seeming most alone,
  Friends are around us, though no word be
    spoken.

Kind messages, that pass from land to land ;
　Kind letters, that betray the heart's deep history,
In which we feel the pressure of a hand, —
　One touch of fire, — and all the rest is mystery !

The pleasant books, that silently among
　Our household treasures take familiar places,
And are to us as if a living tongue
　Spake from the printed leaves or pictured faces !

Perhaps on earth I never shall behold,
　With eye of sense, your outward form and sem-
　　　blance ;
Therefore to me ye never will grow old,
　But live forever young in my remembrance.

Never grow old, nor change, nor pass away !
　Your gentle voices will flow on forever,
When life grows bare and tarnished with decay,
　As through a leafless landscape flows a river.

Not chance of birth or place has made us friends,
　Being oftentimes of different tongues and nations,
But the endeavor for the selfsame ends,
　With the same hopes, and fears, and aspirations.

Therefore I hope to join your seaside walk,
　Saddened, and mostly silent, with emotion ;
Not interrupting with intrusive talk
　The grand, majestic symphonies of ocean.

Therefore I hope, as no unwelcome guest,
  At your warm fireside, when the lamps are
    lighted,
To have my place reserved among the rest,
  Nor stand as one unsought and uninvited!

BY THE SEASIDE

M

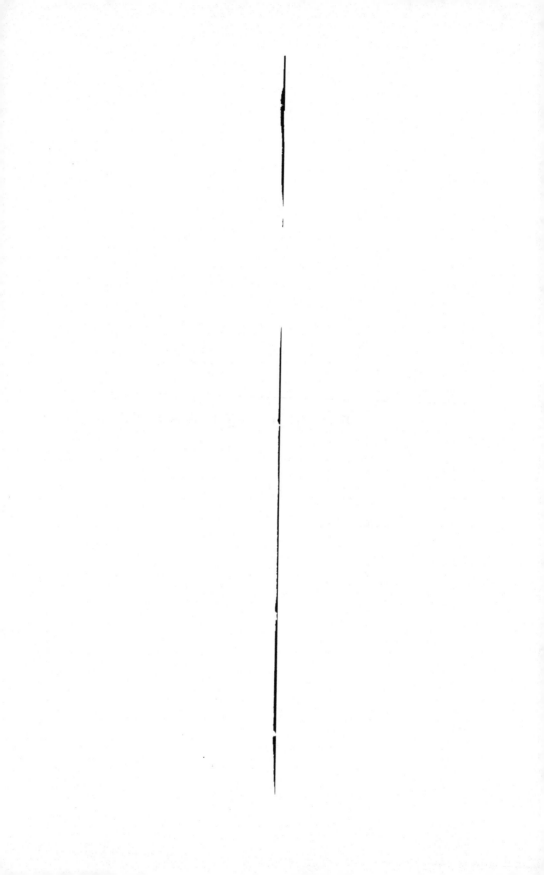

THE BUILDING OF THE SHIP

"BUILD me straight, O worthy Master!
    Stanch and strong, a goodly vessel,
That shall laugh at all disaster,
    And with wave and whirlwind wrestle!"

The merchant's word
Delighted the Master heard;
For his heart was in his work, and the heart
Giveth grace unto every Art.

A quiet smile played round his lips,
As the eddies and dimples of the tide
Play round the bows of ships,
That steadily at anchor ride.
And with a voice that was full of glee,
He answered, " Erelong we will launch
A vessel as goodly, and strong, and stanch,
As ever weathered a wintry sea!"

And first with nicest skill and art,
Perfect and finished in every part,
A little model the Master wrought,
Which should be to the larger plan
What the child is to the man,
Its counterpart in miniature ;
That with a hand more swift and sure
The greater labor might be brought
To answer to his inward thought.
And as he labored, his mind ran o'er
The various ships that were built of yore,
And above them all, and strangest of all
Towered the Great Harry, crank and tall,
Whose picture was hanging on the wall,
With bows and stern raised high in air,
And balconies hanging here and there,
And signal lanterns and flags afloat,
And eight round towers, like those that frown
From some old castle, looking down
Upon the drawbridge and the moat.
And he said with a smile, " Our ship, I wis,
Shall be of another form than this ! " ·

It was of another form, indeed ;
Built for freight, and yet for speed,
A beautiful and gallant craft ;
Broad in the beam, that the stress of the blast,
Pressing down upon sail and mast,
Might not the sharp bows overwhelm ;

Broad in the beam, but sloping aft
With graceful curve and slow degrees,
That she might be docile to the helm,
And that the currents of parted seas,
Closing behind, with mighty force,
Might aid and not impede her course.

In the ship-yard stood the Master,
    With the model of the vessel,
That should laugh at all disaster,
    And with wave and whirlwind wrestle!

Covering many a rood of ground,
Lay the timber piled around ;
Timber of chestnut, and elm, and oak,
And scattered here and there, with these,
The knarred and crooked cedar knees ;
Brought from regions far away,
From Pascagoula's sunny bay,
And the banks of the roaring Roanoke!
Ah! what a wondrous thing it is
To note how many wheels of toil
One thought, one word, can set in motion!
There 's not a ship that sails the ocean,
But every climate, every soil,
Must bring its tribute, great or small,
And help to build the wooden wall!

The sun was rising o'er the sea,

And long the level shadows lay,
As if they, too, the beams would be
Of some great, airy argosy,
Framed and launched in a single day.
That silent architect, the sun,
Had hewn and laid them every one,
Ere the work of man was yet begun.
Beside the Master, when he spoke,
A youth, against an anchor leaning,
Listened, to catch his slightest meaning.
Only the long waves, as they broke
In ripples on the pebbly beach,
Interrupted the old man's speech.

Beautiful they were, in sooth,
The old man and the fiery youth !
The old man, in whose busy brain
Many a ship that sailed the main
Was modelled o'er and o'er again ; —
The fiery youth, who was to be
The heir of his dexterity,
The heir of his house, and his daughter's hand,
When he had built and launched from land
What the elder head had planned.

"Thus," said he, "will we build this ship !
Lay square the blocks upon the slip,
And follow well this plan of mine.
Choose the timbers with greatest care ;

Of all that is unsound beware ;
For only what is sound and strong
To this vessel shall belong.
Cedar of Maine and Georgia pine
Here together shall combine.
A goodly frame, and a goodly fame,
And the UNION be her name !
For the day that gives her to the sea
Shall give my daughter unto thee !"

The Master's word
Enraptured the young man heard ;
And as he turned his face aside,
With a look of joy and a thrill of pride,
Standing before
Her father's door,
He saw the form of his promised bride.
The sun shone on her golden hair,
And her cheek was glowing fresh and fair,
With the breath of morn and the soft sea air.
Like a beauteous barge was she,
Still at rest on the sandy beach,
Just beyond the billow's reach ;
But he
Was the restless, seething, stormy sea !

Ah, how skilful grows the hand
That obeyeth Love's command !
It is the heart, and not the brain,

That to the highest doth attain,
And he who followeth Love's behest
Far excelleth all the rest!

Thus with the rising of the sun
Was the noble task begun,
And soon throughout the ship-yard's bounds
Were heard the intermingled sounds
Of axes and of mallets, plied
With vigorous arms on every side ;
Plied so deftly and so well,
That, ere the shadows of evening fell,
The keel of oak for a noble ship,
Scarfed and bolted, straight and strong,
Was lying ready, and stretched along
The blocks, well placed upon the slip.
Happy, thrice happy, every one
Who sees his labor well begun,
And not perplexed and multiplied,
By idly waiting for time and tide!

And when the hot long day was o'er,
The young man at the Master's door
Sat with the maiden calm and still.
And within the porch, a little more
Removed beyond the evening chill,
The father sat, and told them tales
Of wrecks in the great September gales,
Of pirates coasting the Spanish Main,

And ships that never came back again,
The chance and change of a sailor's life,
Want and plenty, rest and strife,
His roving fancy, like the wind,
That nothing can stay and nothing can bind,
And the magic charm of foreign lands,
With shadows of palms, and shining sands,
Where the tumbling surf,
O'er the coral reefs of Madagascar,
Washes the feet of the swarthy Lascar,
As he lies alone and asleep on the turf.
And the trembling maiden held her breath
At the tales of that awful, pitiless sea,
With all its terror and mystery,
The dim, dark sea, so like unto Death,
That divides and yet unites mankind!
And whenever the old man paused, a gleam
From the bowl of his pipe would awhile illume
The silent group in the twilight gloom,
And thoughtful faces, as in a dream;
And for a moment one might mark
What had been hidden by the dark,
That the head of the maiden lay at rest,
Tenderly, on the young man's breast!

Day by day the vessel grew,
With timbers fashioned strong and true,
Stemson and keelson and sternson-knee,
Till, framed with perfect symmetry,

9*

A skeleton ship rose up to view!
And around the bows and along the side
The heavy hammers and mallets plied,
Till after many a week, at length,
Wonderful for form and strength,
Sublime in its enormous bulk,
Loomed aloft the shadowy hulk!
And around it columns of smoke, upwreathing,
Rose from the boiling, bubbling, seething
Caldron, that glowed,
And overflowed
With the black tar, heated for the sheathing.
And amid the clamors
Of clattering hammers,
He who listened heard now and then
The song of the Master and his men: —

"Build me straight, O worthy Master,
    Stanch and strong, a goodly vessel,
That shall laugh at all disaster,
    And with wave and whirlwind wrestle!"

With oaken brace and copper band,
Lay the rudder on the sand,
That, like a thought, should have control
Over the movement of the whole;
And near it the anchor, whose giant hand
Would reach down and grapple with the land,
And immovable and fast

Hold the great ship against the bellowing blast!
And at the bows an image stood,
By a cunning artist carved in wood,
With robes of white, that far behind
Seemed to be fluttering in the wind.
It was not shaped in a classic mould,
Not like a Nymph or Goddess of old,
Or Naiad rising from the water,
But modelled from the Master's daughter!
On many a dreary and misty night,
'T will be seen by the rays of the signal light,
Speeding along through the rain and the dark,
Like a ghost in its snow-white sark,
The pilot of some phantom bark,
Guiding the vessel, in its flight,
By a path none other knows aright!
Behold, at last,
Each tall and tapering mast
Is swung into its place;
Shrouds and stays
Holding it firm and fast!

Long ago,
In the deer-haunted forests of Maine,
When upon mountain and plain
Lay the snow,
They fell, — those lordly pines!
Those grand, majestic pines!
'Mid shouts and cheers

The jaded steers,
Panting beneath the goad,
Dragged down the weary, winding road
Those captive kings so straight and tall,
To be shorn of their streaming hair,
And, naked and bare,
To feel the stress and the strain
Of the wind and the reeling main,
Whose roar
Would remind them forevermore
Of their native forests they should not see again.

And everywhere
The slender, graceful spars
Poise aloft in the air,
And at the mast-head,
White, blue, and red,
A flag unrolls the stripes and stars.
Ah! when the wanderer, lonely, friendless,
In foreign harbors shall behold
That flag unrolled,
'T will be as a friendly hand
Stretched out from his native land,
Filling his heart with memories sweet and endless!

All is finished! and at length
Has come the bridal day
Of beauty and of strength.
To-day the vessel shall be launched!

With fleecy clouds the sky is blanched,
And o'er the bay,
Slowly, in all his splendors dight,
The great sun rises to behold the sight.

The ocean old,
Centuries old,
Strong as youth, and as uncontrolled,
Paces restless to and fro,
Up and down the sands of gold.
His beating heart is not at rest ;
And far and wide,
With ceaseless flow,
His beard of snow
Heaves with the heaving of his breast.
He waits impatient for his bride.
There she stands,
With her foot upon the sands,
Decked with flags and streamers gay,
In honor of her marriage day,
Her snow-white signals fluttering, blending,
Round her like a veil descending,
Ready to be
The bride of the gray old sea.

On the deck another bride
Is standing by her lover's side.
Shadows from the flags and shrouds,
Like the shadows cast by clouds,

Broken by many a sunny fleck,
Fall around them on the deck.

The prayer is said,
The service read,
The joyous bridegroom bows his head ;
And in tears the good old Master
Shakes the brown hand of his son,
Kisses his daughter's glowing cheek
In silence, for he cannot speak,
And ever faster
Down his own the tears begin to run.
The worthy pastor —
The shepherd of that wandering flock,
That has the ocean for its wold,
That has the vessel for its fold,
Leaping ever from rock to rock —
Spake, with accents mild and clear,
Words of warning, words of cheer,
But tedious to the bridegroom's ear.
He knew the chart
Of the sailor's heart,
All its pleasures and its griefs,
All its shallows and rocky reefs,
All those secret currents, that flow
With such resistless undertow,
And lift and drift, with terrible force,
The will from its moorings and its course.
Therefore he spake, and thus said he : —

" Like unto ships far off at sea,
Outward or homeward bound, are we.
Before, behind, and all around,
Floats and swings the horizon's bound,
Seems at its distant rim to rise
And climb the crystal wall of the skies,
And then again to turn and sink,
As if we could slide from its outer brink.
Ah ! it is not the sea,
It is not the sea that sinks and shelves,
But ourselves
That rock and rise
With endless and uneasy motion,
Now touching the very skies,
Now sinking into the depths of ocean.
Ah ! if our souls but poise and swing
Like the compass in its brazen ring,
Ever level and ever true
To the toil and the task we have to do,
We shall sail securely, and safely reach
The Fortunate Isles, on whose shining beach
The sights we see, and the sounds we hear,
Will be those of joy and not of fear ! "

Then the Master,
With a gesture of command,
Waved his hand ;
And at the word,
Loud and sudden there was heard,

All around them and below,
The sound of hammers, blow on blow,
Knocking away the shores and spurs.
And see! she stirs!
She starts, — she moves, — she seems to feel
The thrill of life along her keel,
And, spurning with her foot the ground,
With one exulting, joyous bound,
She leaps into the ocean's arms!

And lo! from the assembled crowd
There rose a shout, prolonged and loud,
That to the ocean seemed to say,
"Take her, O bridegroom, old and gray,
Take her to thy protecting arms,
With all her youth and all her charms!"

How beautiful she is! How fair
She lies within those arms, that press
Her form with many a soft caress
Of tenderness and watchful care!
Sail forth into the sea, O ship!
Through wind and wave, right onward steer!
The moistened eye, the trembling lip,
Are not the signs of doubt or fear.

Sail forth into the sea of life,
O gentle, loving, trusting wife,
And safe from all adversity

Upon the bosom of that sea
Thy comings and thy goings be!
For gentleness and love and trust
Prevail o'er angry wave and gust;
And in the wreck of noble lives
Something immortal still survives!

Thou, too, sail on, O Ship of State!
Sail on, O UNION, strong and great!
Humanity with all its fears,
With all the hopes of future years,
Is hanging breathless on thy fate!
We know what Master laid thy keel,
What Workmen wrought thy ribs of steel,
Who made each mast, and sail, and rope,
What anvils rang, what hammers beat,
In what a forge and what a heat
Were shaped the anchors of thy hope!
Fear not each sudden sound and shock,
'T is of the wave and not the rock;
'T is but the flapping of the sail,
And not a rent made by the gale!
In spite of rock and tempest's roar,
In spite of false lights on the shore,
Sail on, nor fear to breast the sea!
Our hearts, our hopes, are all with thee,
Our hearts, our hopes, our prayers, our tears,
Our faith triumphant o'er our fears,
Are all with thee, — are all with thee!

THE EVENING STAR

JUST above yon sandy bar,
  As the day grows fainter and dimmer,
Lonely and lovely, a single star
  Lights the air with a dusky glimmer.

Into the ocean faint and far
  Falls the trail of its golden splendor,
And the gleam of that single star
  Is ever refulgent, soft, and tender.

Chrysaor rising out of the sea,
  Showed thus glorious and thus emulous,
Leaving the arms of Callirrhoe,
  · Forever tender, soft, and tremulous.

Thus o'er the ocean faint and far
  Trailed the gleam of his falchion brightly;
Is it a God, or is it a star
  That, entranced, I gaze on nightly!

THE SECRET OF THE SEA

AH ! what pleasant visions haunt me
  As I gaze upon the sea !
All the old romantic legends,
  All my dreams, come back to me.

Sails of silk and ropes of sendal,
  Such as gleam in ancient lore ;
And the singing of the sailors,
  And the answer from the shore !

Most of all, the Spanish ballad
  Haunts me oft, and tarries long,
Of the noble Count Arnaldos
  And the sailor's mystic song.

Like the long waves on a sea-beach,
  Where the sand as silver shines,
With a soft, monotonous cadence,
  Flow its unrhymed lyric lines ; —

Telling how the Count Arnaldos,
  With his hawk upon his hand,
Saw a fair and stately galley,
  Steering onward to the land ; —

How he heard the ancient helmsman
　　Chant a song so wild and clear,
That the sailing sea-bird slowly
　　Poised upon the mast to hear,

Till his soul was full of longing,
　　And he cried, with impulse strong, —
" Helmsman ! for the love of heaven,
　　Teach me, too, that wondrous song ! "

" Wouldst thou," — so the helmsman answered,
　　" Learn the secret of the sea ?
Only those who brave its dangers
　　Comprehend its mystery ! "

In each sail that skims the horizon,
　　In each landward-blowing breeze,
I behold that stately galley,
　　Hear those mournful melodies ;

Till my soul is full of longing
　　For the secret of the sea,
And the heart of the great ocean
　　Sends a thrilling pulse through me.

TWILIGHT

THE twilight is sad and cloudy,
   The wind blows wild and free,
And like the wings of sea-birds
   Flash the white caps of the sea.

But in the fisherman's cottage
   There shines a ruddier light,
And a little face at the window
   Peers out into the night.

Close, close it is pressed to the window,
   As if those childish eyes
Were looking into the darkness,
   To see some form arise.

And a woman's waving shadow
   Is passing to and fro,
Now rising to the ceiling,
   Now bowing and bending low.

What tale do the roaring ocean,
   And the night-wind, bleak and wild,
As they beat at the crazy casement,
   Tell to that little child?

And why do the roaring ocean,
　　And the night-wind, wild and bleak,
As they beat at the heart of the mother,
　　Drive the color from her cheek?

SIR HUMPHREY GILBERT

SOUTHWARD with fleet of ice
　　Sailed the corsair Death;
Wild and fast blew the blast,
　　And the east-wind was his breath.

His lordly ships of ice
　　Glisten in the sun;
On each side, like pennons wide,
　　Flashing crystal streamlets run.

His sails of white sea-mist
　　Dripped with silver rain;
But where he passed there were cast
　　Leaden shadows o'er the main.

Eastward from Campobello
　　Sir Humphrey Gilbert sailed;
Three days or more seaward he bore,
　　Then, alas! the land-wind failed.

Alas! the land-wind failed,
  And ice-cold grew the night;
And never more, on sea or shore,
  Should Sir Humphrey see the light.

He sat upon the deck,
  The Book was in his hand;
" Do not fear! Heaven is as near,"
  He said, " by water as by land! "

In the first watch of the night,
  Without a signal's sound,
Out of the sea, mysteriously,
  The fleet of Death rose all around.

The moon and the evening star
  Were hanging in the shrouds;
Every mast, as it passed,
  Seemed to rake the passing clouds.

They grappled with their prize,
  At midnight black and cold!
As of a rock was the shock;
  Heavily the ground-swell rolled.

Southward through day and dark,
  They drift in close embrace,
With mist and rain, o'er the open main;
  Yet there seems no change of place.

Southward, forever southward,
  They drift through dark and day;
And like a dream, in the Gulf-Stream
  Sinking, vanish all away.

THE LIGHTHOUSE

THE rocky ledge runs far into the sea,
  And on its outer point, some miles away,
The Lighthouse lifts its massive masonry,
  A pillar of fire by night, of cloud by day.

Even at this distance I can see the tides,
  Upheaving, break unheard along its base,
A speechless wrath, that rises and subsides
  In the white lip and tremor of the face.

And as the evening darkens, lo! how bright,
  Through the deep purple of the twilight air,
Beams forth the sudden radiance of its light
  With strange, unearthly splendor in the glare!

Not one alone; from each projecting cape
  And perilous reef along the ocean's verge,
Starts into life a dim, gigantic shape,
  Holding its lantern o'er the restless surge.

Like the great giant Christopher it stands
  Upon the brink of the tempestuous wave,
Wading far out among the rocks and sands,
  The night-o'ertaken mariner to save.

And the great ships sail outward and return,
  Bending and bowing o'er the billowy swells,
And ever joyful, as they see it burn,
  They wave their silent welcomes and farewells.

They come forth from the darkness, and their sails
  Gleam for a moment only in the blaze,
And eager faces, as the light unveils,
  Gaze at the tower, and vanish while they gaze.

The mariner remembers when a child,
  On his first voyage, he saw it fade and sink ;
And when, returning from adventures wild,
  He saw it rise again o'er ocean's brink.

Steadfast, serene, immovable, the same
  Year after year, through all the silent night
Burns on forevermore that quenchless flame,
  Shines on that inextinguishable light !

It sees the ocean to its bosom clasp
  The rocks and sea-sand with the kiss of peace ;
It sees the wild winds lift it in their grasp,
  And hold it up, and shake it like a fleece.

The startled waves leap over it; the storm
   Smites it with all the scourges of the rain,
And steadily against its solid form
   Press the great shoulders of the hurricane.

The sea-bird wheeling round it, with the din
   Of wings and winds and solitary cries,
Blinded and maddened by the light within,
   Dashes himself against the glare, and dies.

A new Prometheus, chained upon the rock,
   Still grasping in his hand the fire of Jove,
It does not hear the cry, nor heed the shock,
   But hails the mariner with words of love.

"Sail on!" it says, "sail on, ye stately ships!
   And with your floating bridge the ocean span;
Be mine to guard this light from all eclipse,
   Be yours to bring man nearer unto man!"

THE FIRE OF DRIFT-WOOD

DEVEREUX FARM, NEAR MARBLEHEAD

WE sat within the farm-house old,
   Whose windows, looking o'er the bay,
Gave to the sea-breeze, damp and cold,
   An easy entrance, night and day.

Not far away we saw the port,
  The strange, old-fashioned, silent town,
The lighthouse, the dismantled fort,
  The wooden houses, quaint and brown.

We sat and talked until the night,
  Descending, filled the little room ;
Our faces faded from the sight,
  Our voices only broke the gloom.

We spake of many a vanished scene,
  Of what we once had thought and said,
Of what had been, and might have been,
  And who was changed, and who was dead ;

And all that fills the hearts of friends,
  When first they feel, with secret pain,
Their lives thenceforth have separate ends,
  And never can be one again ;

The first slight swerving of the heart,
  That words are powerless to express,
And leave it still unsaid in part,
  Or say it in too great excess.

The very tones in which we spake
  Had something strange, I could but mark ;
The leaves of memory seemed to make
  A mournful rustling in the dark.

Oft died the words upon our lips,
  As suddenly, from out the fire
Built of the wreck of stranded ships,
  The flames would leap and then expire.

And, as their splendor flashed and failed,
  We thought of wrecks upon the main,
Of ships dismasted, that were hailed
  And sent no answer back again.

The windows, rattling in their frames,
  The ocean, roaring up the beach,
The gusty blast, the bickering flames,
  All mingled vaguely in our speech ;

Until they made themselves a part
  Of fancies floating through the brain,
The long-lost ventures of the heart,
  That send no answers back again.

O flames that glowed ! O hearts that yearned !
  They were indeed too much akin,
The drift-wood fire without that burned,
  The thoughts that burned and glowed within.

BY THE FIRESIDE

RESIGNATION

THERE is no flock, however watched and
    tended,
  But one dead lamb is there !
There is no fireside, howsoe'er defended,
  But has one vacant chair !

The air is full of farewells to the dying,
  And mournings for the dead ;
The heart of Rachel, for her children crying,
  Will not be comforted !

Let us be patient !   These severe afflictions
  Not from the ground arise,
But oftentimes celestial benedictions
  Assume this dark disguise.

We see but dimly through the mists and vapors ;
  Amid these earthly damps
What seem to us but sad, funereal tapers
  May be heaven's distant lamps.

There is no Death! What seems so is transition;
    This life of mortal breath
Is but a suburb of the life elysian,
    Whose portal we call Death.

She is not dead, — the child of our affection, —
    But gone unto that school
Where she no longer needs our poor protection,
    And Christ himself doth rule.

In that great cloister's stillness and seclusion,
    By guardian angels led,
Safe from temptation, safe from sin's pollution,
    She lives, whom we call dead.

Day after day we think what she is doing
    In those bright realms of air;
Year after year, her tender steps pursuing,
    Behold her grown more fair.

Thus do we walk with her, and keep unbroken
    The bond which nature gives,
Thinking that our remembrance, though unspoken,
    May reach her where she lives.

Not as a child shall we again behold her;
    For when with raptures wild
In our embraces we again enfold her,
    She will not be a child;

But a fair maiden, in her Father's mansion,
  Clothed with celestial grace ;
And beautiful with all the soul's expansion
  Shall we behold her face.

And though at times impetuous with emotion
  And anguish long suppressed,
The swelling heart heaves moaning like the ocean,
  That cannot be at rest, —

We will be patient, and assuage the feeling
  We may not wholly stay ;
By silence sanctifying, not concealing,
  The grief that must have way.

THE BUILDERS

ALL are architects of Fate,
  Working in these walls of Time ;
Some with massive deeds and great,
  Some with ornaments of rhyme.

Nothing useless is, or low ;
  Each thing in its place is best ;
And what seems but idle show
  Strengthens and supports the rest.

For the structure that we raise,
   Time is with materials filled;
Our to-days and yesterdays
   Are the blocks with which we build.

Truly shape and fashion these;
   Leave no yawning gaps between;
Think not, because no man sees,
   Such things will remain unseen.

In the elder days of Art,
   Builders wrought with greatest care
Each minute and unseen part;
   For the Gods see everywhere.

Let us do our work as well,
   Both the unseen and the seen;
Make the house, where Gods may dwell,
   Beautiful, entire, and clean.

Else our lives are incomplete,
   Standing in these walls of Time,
Broken stairways, where the feet
   Stumble as they seek to climb.

Build to-day, then, strong and sure,
   With a firm and ample base;
And ascending and secure
   Shall to-morrow find its place.

Thus alone can we attain
To those turrets, where the eye
Sees the world as one vast plain,
. And one boundless reach of sky.

SAND OF THE DESERT IN AN HOUR-GLASS

A HANDFUL of red sand, from the hot clime
Of Arab deserts brought,
Within this glass becomes the spy of Time,
The minister of Thought.

How many weary centuries has it been
About those deserts blown!
How many strange vicissitudes has seen,
How many histories known!

Perhaps the camels of the Ishmaelite
Trampled and passed it o'er,
When into Egypt from the patriarch's sight
His favorite son they bore.

Perhaps the feet of Moses, burnt and bare,
Crushed it beneath their tread;
Or Pharaoh's flashing wheels into the air
Scattered it as they sped;

Or Mary, with the Christ of Nazareth
    Held close in her caress,
Whose pilgrimage of hope and love and faith
    Illumed the wilderness;

Or anchorites beneath Engaddi's palms
    Pacing the Dead Sea beach,
And singing slow their old Armenian psalms
    In half-articulate speech;

Or caravans, that from Bassora's gate
    With westward steps depart;
Or Mecca's pilgrims, confident of Fate,
    And resolute in heart!

These have passed over it, or may have passed!
    Now in this crystal tower
Imprisoned by some curious hand at last,
    It counts the passing hour.

And as I gaze, these narrow walls expand;
    Before my dreamy eye
Stretches the desert with its shifting sand,
    Its unimpeded sky.

And borne aloft by the sustaining blast,
    This little golden thread
Dilates into a column high and vast,
    A form of fear and dread.

And onward, and across the setting sun,
　　Across the boundless plain,
The column and its broader shadow run,
　　Till thought pursues in vain.

The vision vanishes !　These walls again
　　Shut out the lurid sun,
Shut out the hot, immeasurable plain ;
　　The half-hour's sand is run !

BIRDS OF PASSAGE

BLACK shadows fall
　　From the lindens tall,
That lift aloft their massive wall
　　Against the southern sky ;

And from the realms
Of the shadowy elms
A tide-like darkness overwhelms
　　The fields that round us lie.

But the night is fair,
And everywhere
A warm, soft vapor fills the air,
　　And distant sounds seem near ;

And above, in the light
Of the star-lit night,
Swift birds of passage wing their flight
  Through the dewy atmosphere.

I hear the beat
Of their pinions fleet,
As from the land of snow and sleet
  They seek a southern lea.

I hear the cry
Of their voices high
Falling dreamily through the sky,
  But their forms I cannot see.

O, say not so !
Those sounds that flow
In murmurs of delight and woe
  Come not from wings of birds.

They are the throngs
Of the poet's songs,
Murmurs of pleasures, and pains, and wrongs,
  The sound of winged words.

This is the cry
Of souls, that high
On toiling, beating pinions, fly,
  Seeking a warmer clime.

From their distant flight
Through realms of light
It falls into our world of night,
  With the murmuring sound of rhyme.

THE OPEN WINDOW

THE old house by the lindens
    Stood silent in the shade,
And on the gravelled pathway
  The light and shadow played.

I saw the nursery windows
  Wide open to the air ;
But the faces of the children,
  They were no longer there.

The large Newfoundland house-dog
  Was standing by the door ;
He looked for his little playmates,
  Who would return no more.

They walked not under the lindens,
  They played not in the hall ;
But shadow, and silence, and sadness
  Were hanging over all.

The birds sang in the branches,
  With sweet, familiar tone;
But the voices of the children
  Will be heard in dreams alone!

And the boy that walked beside me,
  He could not understand
Why closer in mine, ah! closer,
  I pressed his warm, soft hand!

KING WITLAF'S DRINKING–HORN

WITLAF, a king of the Saxons,
    Ere yet his last he breathed,
To the merry monks of Croyland
  His drinking-horn bequeathed, —

That, whenever they sat at their revels,
  And drank from the golden bowl,
They might remember the donor,
  And breathe a prayer for his soul.

So sat they once at Christmas,
  And bade the goblet pass;
In their beards the red wine glistened
  Like dew-drops in the grass.

They drank to the soul of Witlaf,
    They drank to Christ the Lord,
And to each of the Twelve Apostles,
    Who had preached his holy word.

They drank to the Saints and Martyrs
    Of the dismal days of yore,
And as soon as the horn was empty
    They remembered one Saint more.

And the reader droned from the pulpit,
    Like the murmur of many bees,
The legend of good Saint Guthlac,
    And Saint Basil's homilies ;

Till the great bells of the convent,
    From their prison in the tower,
Guthlac and Bartholomæus,
    Proclaimed the midnight hour.

And the Yule-log cracked in the chimney,
    And the Abbot bowed his head,
And the flamelets flapped and flickered,
    But the Abbot was stark and dead.

Yet still in his pallid fingers
    He clutched the golden bowl,
In which, like a pearl dissolving,
    Had sunk and dissolved his soul.

But not for this their revels
  The jovial monks forbore,
For they cried, " Fill high the goblet !
  We must drink to one Saint more ! "

GASPAR BECERRA

BY his evening fire the artist
  Pondered o'er his secret shame ;
Baffled, weary, and disheartened,
  Still he mused, and dreamed of fame.

'T was an image of the Virgin
  That had tasked his utmost skill ;
But alas ! his fair ideal
  Vanished and escaped him still.

From a distant Eastern island
  Had the precious wood been brought ;
Day and night the anxious master
  At his toil untiring wrought ;

Till, discouraged and desponding,
  Sat he now in shadows deep,
And the day's humiliation
  Found oblivion in sleep.

Then a voice cried, " Rise, O master!
  From the burning brand of oak
Shape the thought that stirs within thee ! "
  And the startled artist woke, —

Woke, and from the smoking embers
  Seized and quenched the glowing wood ;
And therefrom he carved an image,
  And he saw that it was good.

O thou sculptor, painter, poet !
  Take this lesson to thy heart :
That is best which lieth nearest ;
  Shape from that thy work of art.

PEGASUS IN POUND

ONCE into a quiet village,
  Without haste and without heed,
In the golden prime of morning,
  Strayed the poet's winged steed.

It was Autumn, and incessant
  Piped the quails from shocks and sheaves,
And, like living coals, the apples
  Burned among the withering leaves.

Loud the clamorous bell was ringing
   From its belfry gaunt and grim ;
'T was the daily call to labor,
   Not a triumph meant for him.

Not the less he saw the landscape,
   In its gleaming vapor veiled ;
Not the less he breathed the odors
   That the dying leaves exhaled.

Thus, upon the village common,
   By the school-boys he was found ;
And the wise men, in their wisdom,
   Put him straightway into pound.

Then the sombre village crier,
   Ringing loud his brazen bell,
Wandered down the street proclaiming
   There was an estray to sell.

And the curious country people,
   Rich and poor, and young and old,
Came in haste to see this wondrous
   Winged steed, with mane of gold.

Thus the day passed, and the evening
   Fell, with vapors cold and dim ;
But it brought no food nor shelter,
   Brought no straw nor stall, for him.

Patiently, and still expectant,
   Looked he through the wooden bars,
Saw the moon rise o'er the landscape,
   Saw the tranquil, patient stars ;

Till at length the bell at midnight
   Sounded from its dark abode,
And, from out a neighboring farm-yard,
   Loud the cock Alectryon crowed.

Then, with nostrils wide distended,
   Breaking from his iron chain,
And unfolding far his pinions,
   To those stars he soared again.

On the morrow, when the village
   Woke to all its toil and care,
Lo! the strange steed had departed,
   And they knew not when nor where.

But they found, upon the greensward
   Where his struggling hoofs had trod,
Pure and bright, a fountain flowing
   From the hoof-marks in the sod.

From that hour, the fount unfailing
   Gladdens the whole region round,
Strengthening all who drink its waters,
   While it soothes them with its sound.

TEGNÉR'S DRAPA

I HEARD a voice, that cried,
　"Balder the Beautiful
Is dead, is dead!"
And through the misty air
Passed like the mournful cry
Of sunward sailing cranes.

I saw the pallid corpse
Of the dead sun
Borne through the Northern sky.
Blasts from Niffelheim
Lifted the sheeted mists
Around him as he passed.

And the voice forever cried,
"Balder the Beautiful
Is dead, is dead!"
And died away
Through the dreary night,
In accents of despair.

Balder the Beautiful,
God of the summer sun,
Fairest of all the Gods!
Light from his forehead beamed,

Rûnes were upon his tongue,
As on the warrior's sword.

All things in earth and air
Bound were by magic spell
Never to do him harm ;
Even the plants and stones ;
All save the mistletoe,
The sacred mistletoe !

Hœder, the blind old God,
Whose feet are shod with silence,
Pierced through that gentle breast
With his sharp spear, by fraud
Made of the mistletoe,
The accursed mistletoe !

They laid him in his ship,
With horse and harness,
As on a funeral pyre.
Odin placed
A ring upon his finger,
And whispered in his ear.

They launched the burning ship !
It floated far away
Over the misty sea,
Till like the sun it seemed,
Sinking beneath the waves.
Balder returned no more !

So perish the old Gods !
But out of the sea of Time
Rises a new land of song,
Fairer than the old.
Over its meadows green
Walk the young bards and sing.

Build it again,
O ye bards,
Fairer than before !
Ye fathers of the new race,
Feed upon morning dew,
Sing the new Song of Love !

The law of force is dead !
The law of love prevails !
Thor, the thunderer,
Shall rule the earth no more,
No more, with threats,
Challenge the meek Christ.

Sing no more,
O ye bards of the North,
Of Vikings and of Jarls !
Of the days of Eld
Preserve the freedom only,
Not the deeds of blood !

SONNET

ON MRS. KEMBLE'S READINGS FROM SHAKESPEARE

O PRECIOUS evenings! all too swiftly sped!
　Leaving us heirs to amplest heritages
Of all the best thoughts of the greatest sages,
And giving tongues unto the silent dead!
How our hearts glowed and trembled as she read,
　Interpreting by tones the wondrous pages
　Of the great poet who foreruns the ages,
　Anticipating all that shall be said!
O happy Reader! having for thy text
　The magic book, whose Sibylline leaves have
　　　caught
　The rarest essence of all human thought!
O happy Poet! by no critic vext!
　How must thy listening spirit now rejoice
　To be interpreted by such a voice!

THE SINGERS

GOD sent his Singers upon earth
　With songs of sadness and of mirth,
That they might touch the hearts of men,
And bring them back to heaven again.

The first, a youth, with soul of fire,
Held in his hand a golden lyre ;
Through groves he wandered, and by streams,
Playing the music of our dreams.

The second, with a bearded face,
Stood singing in the market-place,
And stirred with accents deep and loud
The hearts of all the listening crowd.

A gray old man, the third and last,
Sang in cathedrals dim and vast,
While the majestic organ rolled
Contrition from its mouths of gold.

And those who heard the Singers three
Disputed which the best might be ;
For still their music seemed to start
Discordant echoes in each heart.

But the great Master said, " I see
No best in kind, but in degree ;
I gave a various gift to each,
To charm, to strengthen, and to teach.

" These are the three great chords of might,
And he whose ear is tuned aright
Will hear no discord in the three,
But the most perfect harmony."

SUSPIRIA

TAKE them, O Death! and bear away
Whatever thou canst call thine own!
Thine image, stamped upon this clay,
Doth give thee that, but that alone!

Take them, O Grave! and let them lie
Folded upon thy narrow shelves,
As garments by the soul laid by,
And precious only to ourselves!

Take them, O great Eternity!
Our little life is but a gust
That bends the branches of thy tree,
And trails its blossoms in the dust!

HYMN

FOR MY BROTHER'S ORDINATION

CHRIST to the young man said: "Yet one
thing more;
If thou wouldst perfect be,
Sell all thou hast and give it to the poor,
And come and follow me!"

Within this temple Christ again, unseen,
  Those sacred words hath said,
And his invisible hands to-day have been
  Laid on a young man's head.

And evermore beside him on his way
  The unseen Christ shall move,
That he may lean upon his arm and say,
  "Dost thou, dear Lord, approve?"

Beside him at the marriage feast shall be,
  To make the scene more fair;
Beside him in the dark Gethsemane
  Of pain and midnight prayer.

O holy trust! O endless sense of rest!
  Like the beloved John
To lay his head upon the Saviour's breast,
  And thus to journey on!

THE

BLIND GIRL OF CASTÈL-CUILLÈ

FROM THE GASCON OF JASMIN

ONLY the Lowland tongue of Scotland might
Rehearse this little tragedy aright;
Let me attempt it with an English quill;
And take, O Reader, for the deed the will.

THE BLIND GIRL OF CASTÈL-CUILLÈ

FROM THE GASCON OF JASMIN

I.

AT the foot of the mountain height
  Where is perched Castèl-Cuillè,
When the apple, the plum, and the almond tree
  In the plain below were growing white,
  This is the song one might perceive
On a Wednesday morn of Saint Joseph's Eve :

"The roads should blossom, the roads should
   bloom,
So fair a bride shall leave her home !
Should blossom and bloom with garlands gay,
So fair a bride shall pass to-day !"

This old Te Deum, rustic rites attending,
  Seemed from the clouds descending;
  When lo ! a merry company
Of rosy village girls, clean as the eye,
  Each one with her attendant swain,
Came to the cliff, all singing the same strain ;
Resembling there, so near unto the sky,

Rejoicing angels, that kind Heaven has sent
For their delight and our encouragement.
      Together blending,
      And soon descending
      The narrow sweep
      Of the hillside steep,
      They wind aslant
      Towards Saint Amant,
      Through leafy alleys
      Of verdurous valleys
      With merry sallies
      Singing their chant :

"The roads should blossom, the roads should
    bloom,
So fair a bride shall leave her home !
Should blossom and bloom with garlands gay,
So fair a bride shall pass to-day!"

It is Baptiste, and his affianced maiden,
With garlands for the bridal laden !

The sky was blue ; without one cloud of gloom,
  The sun of March was shining brightly,
And to the air the freshening wind gave lightly
  Its breathings of perfume.

When one beholds the dusky hedges blossom,
A rustic bridal, ah ! how sweet it is !

To sounds of joyous melodies,
That touch with tenderness the trembling bosom,
      A band of maidens
      Gayly frolicking,
      A band of youngsters
      Wildly rollicking!
        Kissing,
        Caressing,
     With fingers pressing,
      Till in the veriest
   Madness of mirth, as they dance,
   They retreat and advance,
     Trying whose laugh shall be loudest
       and merriest ;
  While the bride, with roguish eyes,
Sporting with them, now escapes and cries :
  " Those who catch me
     Married verily
     This year shall be ! "

   And all pursue with eager haste,
   And all attain what they pursue,
And touch her pretty apron fresh and new,
   And the linen kirtle round her waist.

   Meanwhile, whence comes it that among
   These youthful maidens fresh and fair,
   So joyous, with such laughing air,
   Baptiste stands sighing, with silent tongue?

11 *

And yet the bride is fair and young !
Is it Saint Joseph would say to us all,
That love, o'er-hasty, precedeth a fall?
    O no ! for a maiden frail, I trow,
    Never bore so lofty a brow !
What lovers ! they give not a single caress !
To see them so careless and cold to-day,
    These are grand people, one would say.
What ails Baptiste? what grief doth him oppress?

    It is, that, half-way up the hill,
    In yon cottage, by whose walls
    Stand the cart-house and the stalls,
    Dwelleth the blind orphan still,
    Daughter of a veteran old ;
    And you must know, one year ago,
    That Margaret, the young and tender,
    Was the village pride and splendor,
    And Baptiste her lover bold.
    Love, the deceiver, them ensnared ;
    For them the altar was prepared ;
    But alas ! the summer's blight,
    The dread disease that none can stay,
    The pestilence that walks by night,
    Took the young bride's sight away.

All at the father's stern command was changed ;
Their peace was gone, but not their love estranged.
Wearied at home, erelong the lover fled ;

Returned but three short days ago,
The golden chain they round him throw,
He is enticed, and onward led
To marry Angela, and yet
Is thinking ever of Margaret.

Then suddenly a maiden cried,
" Anna, Theresa, Mary, Kate !
Here comes the cripple Jane ! "   And by a foun-
        tain's side
A woman, bent and gray with years,
Under the mulberry-trees appears,
And all towards her run, as fleet
As had they wings upon their feet.

It is that Jane, the cripple Jane,
Is a soothsayer, wary and kind.
She telleth fortunes, and none complain.
    She promises one a village swain,
    Another a happy wedding-day,
    And the bride a lovely boy straightway.
All comes to pass as she avers ;
She never deceives, she never errs.

But for this once the village seer
Wears a countenance severe,
And from beneath her eyebrows thin and white
    Her two eyes flash like cannons bright
    Aimed at the bridegroom in waistcoat blue,

Who, like a statue, stands in view;
Changing color, as well he might,
When the beldame wrinkled and gray
Takes the young bride by the hand,
And, with the tip of her reedy wand
Making the sign of the cross, doth say :—
" Thoughtless Angela, beware !
Lest, when thou weddest this false bridegroom,
Thou diggest for thyself a tomb ! "
And she was silent ; and the maidens fair
Saw from each eye escape a swollen tear ;
But on a little streamlet silver-clear,
What are two drops of turbid rain ?
Saddened a moment, the bridal train
Resumed the dance and song again ;
The bridegroom only was pale with fear ; —
And down green alleys
Of verdurous valleys,
With merry sallies,
They sang the refrain :—

" The roads should blossom, the roads should
    bloom,
So fair a bride shall leave her home !
Should blossom and bloom with garlands gay,
So fair a bride shall pass to-day ! "

II.

AND by suffering worn and weary,
   But beautiful as some fair angel yet,
    Thus lamented Margaret,
   In her cottage lone and dreary :—

"He has arrived! arrived at last!
Yet Jane has named him not these three days past,
   Arrived! yet keeps aloof so far!
And knows that of my night he is the star!
Knows that long months I wait alone, benighted,
And count the moments since he went away!
Come! keep the promise of that happier day,
That I may keep the faith to thee I·plighted!
What joy have I without thee? what delight?
Grief wastes my life, and makes it misery;
Day for the others ever, but for me
   Forever night! forever night!
When he is gone 't is dark! my soul is sad!
I suffer! O my God! come, make me glad.
When he is near, no thoughts of day intrude;
Day has blue heavens, but Baptiste has blue eyes!
Within them shines for me a heaven of love,
A heaven all happiness, like that above,
   No more of grief! no more of lassitude!

Earth I forget, — and heaven, and all distresses,
When seated by my side my hand he presses ;
    But when alone, remember all !
Where is Baptiste ? he hears not when I call !
A branch of ivy, dying on the ground,
    I need some bough to twine around !
In pity come ! be to my suffering kind !
True love, they say, in grief doth more abound !
    What then — when one is blind ?

    "Who knows ? perhaps I am forsaken !
Ah ! woe is me ! then bear me to my grave !
    O God ! what thoughts within me waken !
Away ! he will return ! I do but rave !
    He will return ! I need not fear !
    He swore it by our Saviour dear ;
    He could not come at his own will ;
    Is weary, or perhaps is ill !
    Perhaps his heart, in this disguise,
    Prepares for me some sweet surprise !
But some one comes ! Though blind, my heart
        can see !
And that deceives me not ! 't is he ! 't is he !"

    And the door ajar is set,
    And poor, confiding Margaret
Rises, with outstretched arms, but sightless eyes ;
'T is only Paul, her brother, who thus cries : —

" Angela the bride has passed !
I saw the wedding guests go by ;
Tell me, my sister, why were we not asked ?
For all are there but you and I ! "

" Angela married ! and not send
To tell her secret unto me !
O, speak ! who may the bridegroom be ? "
" My sister, 't is Baptiste, thy friend ! "

A cry the blind girl gave, but nothing said ;
A milky whiteness spreads upon her cheeks ;
An icy hand, as heavy as lead,
Descending, as her brother speaks,
Upon her heart, that has ceased to beat,
Suspends awhile its life and heat.
She stands beside the boy, now sore distressed,
A wax Madonna as a peasant dressed.

At length, the bridal song again
Brings her back to her sorrow and pain.

" Hark ! the joyous airs are ringing !
Sister, dost thou hear them singing?
How merrily they laugh and jest !
Would we were bidden with the rest !
I would don my hose of homespun gray,
And my doublet of linen striped and gay ;
Perhaps they will come ; for they do not wed

Till to-morrow at seven o'clock, it is said!"
"I know it!" answered Margaret;
Whom the vision, with aspect black as jet,
Mastered again; and its hand of ice
Held her heart crushed, as in a vice!
"Paul, be not sad! 'T is a holiday;
To-morrow put on thy doublet gay!
But leave me now for a while alone."
Away, with a hop and a jump, went Paul,
And, as he whistled along the hall,
Entered Jane, the crippled crone.

"Holy Virgin! what dreadful heat!
I am faint, and weary, and out of breath!
But thou art cold, — art chill as death;
My little friend! what ails thee, sweet?"
"Nothing! I heard them singing home the bride;
And, as I listened to the song,
I thought my turn would come erelong,
Thou knowest it is at Whitsuntide.
Thy cards forsooth can never lie,
To me such joy they prophesy,
Thy skill shall be vaunted far and wide
When they behold him at my side.
And poor Baptiste, what sayest thou?
It must seem long to him; — methinks I see him
now!"
Jane, shuddering, her hand doth press:
"Thy love I cannot all approve;

We must not trust too much to happiness ; —
Go, pray to God, that thou mayst love him less ! "
  " The more I pray, the more I love !
It is no sin, for God is on my side ! "
It was enough ; and Jane no more replied.

Now to all hope her heart is barred and cold ;
    But to deceive the beldame old
    She takes a sweet, contented air ;
    Speak of foul weather or of fair,
    At every word the maiden smiles !
    Thus the beguiler she beguiles ;
So that, departing at the evening's close,
    She says, " She may be saved ! she nothing
        knows ! "

    Poor Jane, the cunning sorceress !
Now that thou wouldst, thou art no prophetess !
This morning, in the fulness of thy heart,
    Thou wast so, far beyond thine art !

                I I I.

NOW rings the bell, nine times reverberating,
    And the white daybreak, stealing up the sky,
Sees in two cottages two maidens waiting,
        How differently !

Queen of a day, by flatterers caressed,
    The one puts on her cross and crown,
    Decks with a huge bouquet her breast,
    And flaunting, fluttering up and down,
    Looks at herself, and cannot rest.
    The other, blind, within her little room,
    Has neither crown nor flower's perfume ;
But in their stead for something gropes apart,
    That in a drawer's recess doth lie,
And, 'neath her bodice of bright scarlet dye,
    Convulsive clasps it to her heart.

    The one, fantastic, light as air,
       'Mid kisses ringing,
       And joyous singing,
    Forgets to say her morning prayer !

The other, with cold drops upon her brow,
    Joins her two hands, and kneels upon the floor,
And whispers, as her brother opes the door,
    " O God ! forgive me now ! "

    And then the orphan, young and blind,
    Conducted by her brother's hand,
    Towards the church, through paths unscanned,
    With tranquil air, her way doth wind.
Odors of laurel, making her faint and pale,
    Round her at times exhale,
And in the sky as yet no sunny ray,
    But brumal vapors gray.

Near that castle, fair to see,
Crowded with sculptures old, in every part,
   Marvels of nature and of art,
      And proud of its name of high degree,
   A little chapel, almost bare
   At the base of the rock, is builded there ;
   All glorious that it lifts aloof,
   Above each jealous cottage roof,
Its sacred summit, swept by autumn gales,
   And its blackened steeple high in air,
   Round which the osprey screams and sails.

   " Paul, lay thy noisy rattle by ! "
Thus Margaret said. " Where are we ? we as-
      cend ! "
   " Yes ; seest thou not our journey's end ?
Hearest not the osprey from the belfry cry ?
The hideous bird, that brings ill luck, we know !
Dost thou remember when our father said,
   The night we watched beside his bed,
   ' O daughter, I am weak and low ;
Take care of Paul ; I feel that I am dying ! '
And thou, and he, and I, all fell to crying ?
Then on the roof the osprey screamed aloud ;
And here they brought our father in his shroud.
There is his grave ; there stands the cross we set ;
Why dost thou clasp me so, dear Margaret ?
   Come in ! The bride will be here soon :
Thou tremblest ! O my God ! thou art going to
      swoon ! "

She could no more, — the blind girl, weak and
    weary !
A voice seemed crying from that grave so dreary,
"What wouldst thou do, my daughter?"— and she
    started ;
    And quick recoiled, aghast, faint-hearted ;
But Paul, impatient, urges evermore
    Her steps towards the open door ;
And when, beneath her feet, the unhappy maid
Crushes the laurel near the house immortal,
And with her head, as Paul talks on again,
    Touches the crown of filigrane
    Suspended from the low-arched portal,
    No more restrained, no more afraid,
    She walks, as for a feast arrayed,
And in the ancient chapel's sombre night
    They both are lost to sight.

      At length the bell,
      With booming sound,
      Sends forth, resounding round,
Its hymeneal peal o'er rock and down the dell.
    It is broad day, with sunshine and with rain ;
      And yet the guests delay not long,
      For soon arrives the bridal train,
      And with it brings the village throng.

In sooth, deceit maketh no mortal gay,
For lo ! Baptiste on this triumphant day,

Mute as an idiot, sad as yester-morning,
Thinks only of the beldame's words of warning.

And Angela thinks of her cross, I wis;
To be a bride is all! The pretty lisper
Feels her heart swell to hear all round her whisper,
" How beautiful! how beautiful she is!"

But she must calm that giddy head,
For already the Mass is said;
At the holy table stands the priest;
The wedding ring is blessed; Baptiste receives it;
Ere on the finger of the bride he leaves it,
He must pronounce one word at least!
'T is spoken; and sudden at the groomsman's side
" 'T is he!" a well-known voice has cried.
And while the wedding guests all hold their breath,
Opes the confessional, and the blind girl, see!
" Baptiste," she said, " since thou hast wished my
death,
As holy water be my blood for thee!"
And calmly in the air a knife suspended!
Doubtless her guardian angel near attended,
For anguish did its work so well,
That, ere the fatal stroke descended,
Lifeless she fell!

At eve, instead of bridal verse,
The De Profundis filled the air;

Decked with flowers a simple hearse
To the churchyard forth they bear;
Village girls in robes of snow
Follow, weeping as they go;
Nowhere was a smile that day,
No, ah no! for each one seemed to say:—

"The road should mourn and be veiled in gloom,
So fair a corpse shall leave its home!
Should mourn and should weep, ah, well-away!
So fair a corpse shall pass to-day!"

A CHRISTMAS CAROL

FROM THE NOEI BOURGUIGNON DE GUI BARÔZAI

I HEAR along our street
　　Pass the minstrel throngs;
Hark! they play so sweet,
On their hautboys, Christmas songs!
　　Let us by the fire
　　Ever higher
Sing them till the night expire!

　　In December ring
　　Every day the chimes;

Loud the gleemen sing
In the streets their merry rhymes.
　　Let us by the fire
　　Ever higher
Sing them till the night expire.

　　Shepherds at the grange,
　　Where the Babe was born,
　　Sang, with many a change,
Christmas carols until morn.
　　Let us by the fire
　　Ever higher
Sing them till the night expire !

　　These good people sang
　　Songs devout and sweet ;
　　While the rafters rang,
There they stood with freezing feet.
　　Let us by the fire
　　Ever higher
Sing them till the night expire.

　　Nuns in frigid cells
　　At this holy tide,
　　For want of something else,
Christmas songs at times have tried.
　　Let us by the fire
　　Ever higher
Sing them till the night expire !

Washerwomen old,
To the sound they beat,
Sing by rivers cold,
With uncovered heads and feet.
Let us by the fire
Ever higher
Sing them till the night expire.

Who by the fireside stands
Stamps his feet and sings ;
But he who blows his hands
Not so gay a carol brings.
Let us by the fire
Ever higher
Sing them till the night expire !

NOTES

NOTES

Page 8. *All the Foresters of Flanders.*

The title of Foresters was given to the early governors of Flanders, appointed by the kings of France. Lyderick du Bucq, in the days of Clotaire the Second, was the first of them ; and Beaudoin Bras-de-Fer, who stole away the fair Judith, daughter of Charles the Bald, from the French court, and married her in Bruges, was the last. After him the title of Forester was changed to that of Count. Philippe d'Alsace, Guy de Dampierre, and Louis de Crécy, coming later in the order of time, were therefore rather Counts than Foresters. Philippe went twice to the Hóly Land as a Crusader, and died of the plague at St. Jean-d'Acre, shortly after the capture of the city by the Christians. Guy de Dampierre died in the prison of Compiègne. Louis de Crécy was son and successor of Robert de Béthune, who strangled his wife, Yolande de Bourgogne, with the bridle of his horse, for having poisoned, at the age of eleven years, Charles, his son by his first wife, Blanche d'Anjou.

Page 9. *Stately dames, like queens attended.*

When Philippe-le-Bel, king of France, visited Flanders with his queen, she was so astonished at the magnificence of the dames of Bruges, that she exclaimed : " Je croyais être seule reine ici, mais il paraît que ceux de Flandre qui se trouvent dans nos prisons sont tous des princes, car leurs femmes sont habillées comme des princesses et des reines."

When the burgomasters of Ghent, Bruges, and Ypres went to Paris to pay homage to King John, in 1351, they were received with great pomp and distinction; but, being invited to a festival, they observed that their seats at table were not furnished with cushions; whereupon, to make known their displeasure at this want of regard to their dignity, they folded their richly embroidered cloaks and seated themselves upon them. On rising from table, they left their cloaks behind them, and, being informed of their apparent forgetfulness, Simon van Eertrycke, burgomaster of Bruges, replied, "We Flemings are not in the habit of carrying away our cushions after dinner."

Page 9. *Knights who bore the Fleece of Gold.*

Philippe de Bourgogne, surnamed Le Bon, espoused Isabella of Portugal, on the 10th of January, 1430; and on the same day instituted the famous order of the Fleece of Gold.

Page 9. *I beheld the gentle Mary.*

Marie de Valois, Duchess of Burgundy, was left by the death of her father, Charles-le-Téméraire, at the age of twenty, the richest heiress of Europe. She came to Bruges, as Countess of Flanders, in 1477, and in the same year was married by proxy to the Archduke Maximilian. According to the custom of the time, the Duke of Bavaria, Maximilian's substitute, slept with the princess. They were both in complete dress, separated by a naked sword, and attended by four armed guards. Marie was adored by her subjects for her gentleness and her many other virtues.

Maximilian was son of the Emperor Frederick the Third, and is the same person mentioned afterwards in the poem of *Nuremberg* as the Kaiser Maximilian, and the hero of Pfinzing's poem of *Teuerdank*. Having been imprisoned by the revolted burghers of Bruges, they refused to release him,

till he consented to kneel in the public square, and to swear
on the Holy Evangelists and the body of Saint Donatus, that
he would not take vengeance upon them for their rebellion.

Page 9. *The bloody battle of the Spurs of Gold.*

This battle, the most memorable in Flemish history, was
fought under the walls of Courtray, on the 11th of July, 1302,
between the French and the Flemings, the former commanded
by Robert, Comte d'Artois, and the latter by Guillaume de
Juliers, and Jean, Comte de Namur. The French army was
completely routed, with a loss of twenty thousand infantry and
seven thousand cavalry; among whom were sixty-three princes,
dukes, and counts, seven hundred lords-banneret, and eleven
hundred noblemen. The flower of the French nobility perished on that day; to which history has given the name of the
Journée des Éperons d'Or, from the great number of golden
spurs found on the field of battle. Seven hundred of them
were hung up as a trophy in the church of Notre Dame de
Courtray; and, as the cavaliers of that day wore but a single
spur each, these vouched to God for the violent and bloody
death of seven hundred of his creatures.

Page 9. *Saw the fight at Minnewater.*

When the inhabitants of Bruges were digging a canal at
Minnewater, to bring the waters of the Lys from Deynze to
their city, they were attacked and routed by the citizens of
Ghent, whose commerce would have been much injured by
the canal. They were led by Jean Lyons, captain of a milita-
ry company at Ghent, called the *Chaperons Blancs*. He had
great sway over the turbulent populace, who, in those prosper-
ous times of the city, gained an easy livelihood by laboring two
or three days in the week, and had the remaining four or five
to devote to public affairs. The fight at Minnewater was followed by open rebellion against Louis de Maele, the Count of

Flanders and Protector of Bruges. His superb château of Wondelghem was pillaged and burnt; and the insurgents forced the gates of Bruges, and entered in triumph, with Lyons mounted at their head. A few days afterwards he died suddenly, perhaps by poison.

Meanwhile the insurgents received a check at the village of Nevèle; and two hundred of them perished in the church, which was burned by the Count's orders. One of the chiefs, Jean de Lannoy, took refuge in the belfry. From the summit of the tower he held forth his purse filled with gold, and begged for deliverance. It was in vain. His enemies cried to him from below to save himself as best he might; and, half suffocated with smoke and flame, he threw himself from the tower and perished at their feet. Peace was soon afterwards established, and the Count retired to faithful Bruges.

Page 9. *The Golden Dragon's nest.*

The Golden Dragon, taken from the church of St. Sophia, at Constantinople, in one of the Crusades, and placed on the belfry of Bruges, was afterwards transported to Ghent by Philip van Artevelde, and still adorns the belfry of that city.

The inscription on the alarm-bell at Ghent is, "*Mynen naem is Roland; als ik klep is er brand, and als ik luy is er victorie in het land.*" My name is Roland; when I toll there is fire, and when I ring there is victory in the land.

Page 18. *That their great imperial city stretched its hand through every clime.*

An old popular proverb of the town runs thus: —

> "*Nürnberg's Hand*
> *Geht durch alle Land.*"
> Nuremberg's hand
> Goes through every land.

Page 19. *Sat the poet Melchior singing Kaiser Maximilian's praise.*

Melchior Pfinzing was one of the most celebrated German poets of the sixteenth century. The hero of his *Teuerdank* was the reigning emperor, Maximilian; and the poem was to the Germans of that day what the *Orlando Furioso* was to the Italians. Maximilian is mentioned before, in the *Belfry of Bruges.* See page 268.

Page 19. *In the church of sainted Sebald sleeps enshrined his holy dust.*

The tomb of Saint Sebald, in the church which bears his name, is one of the richest works of art in Nuremberg. It is of bronze, and was cast by Peter Vischer and his sons, who labored upon it thirteen years. It is adorned with nearly one hundred figures, among which those of the Twelve Apostles are conspicuous for size and beauty.

Page 19. *In the church of sainted Lawrence stands a pix of sculpture rare.*

This pix, or tabernacle for the vessels of the sacrament, is by the hand of Adam Kraft. It is an exquisite piece of sculpture in white stone, and rises to the height of sixty-four feet. It stands in the choir, whose richly painted windows cover it with varied colors.

Page 21. *Wisest of the Twelve Wise Masters.*

The Twelve Wise Masters was the title of the original corporation of the Mastersingers. Hans Sachs, the cobbler of Nuremberg, though not one of the original Twelve, was the most renowned of the Mastersingers, as well as the most voluminous. He flourished in the sixteenth century; and left behind him thirty-four folio volumes of manuscript, containing two hundred and eight plays, one thousand and seven hundred comic tales, and between four and five thousand lyric poems.

Page 21. *As in Adam Puschman's song.*

Adam Puschman, in his poem on the death of Hans Sachs, describes him as he appeared in a vision : —

> "An old man,
> Gray and white, and dove-like,
> Who had, in sooth, a great beard,
> And read in a fair, great book,
> Beautiful with golden clasps."

Page 36. *The Occultation of Orion.*

Astronomically speaking, this title is incorrect; as I apply to a constellation what can properly be applied to some of its stars only.   But my observation is made from the hill of song, and not from that of science ; and will, I trust, be found sufficiently accurate for the present purpose.

Page 44. *Who, unharmed, on his tusks once caught the bolts of the thunder.*

"A delegation of warriors from the Delaware tribe having visited the governor of Virginia, during the Revolution, on matters of business, after these had been discussed and settled in council, the governor asked them some questions relative to their country, and among others, what they knew or had heard of the animal whose bones were found at the Saltlicks on the Ohio.   Their chief speaker immediately put himself into an attitude of oratory, and with a pomp suited to what he conceived the elevation of his subject, informed him that it was a tradition handed down from their fathers, 'that in ancient times a herd of these tremendous animals came to the Big-bone licks, and began an universal destruction of the bear, deer, elks, buffaloes, and other animals which had been created for the use of the Indians: that the Great Man above, looking

down and seeing this, was so enraged, that he seized his lightning, descended on the earth, seated himself on a neighboring
mountain, on a rock of which his seat and the print of his
feet are still to be seen, and hurled his bolts among them
till the whole were slaughtered, except the big bull, who,
presenting his forehead to the shafts, shook them off as they
fell; but missing one at length, it wounded him in the side;
whereon, springing round, he bounded over the Ohio, over
the Wabash, the Illinois, and finally over the great lakes,
where he is living at this day.'" — JEFFERSON'S *Notes on Virginia*, Query VI.

Page 55. *Walter von der Vogelweid.*

Walter von der Vogelweid, or Bird-Meadow was one of
the principal Minnesingers of the thirteenth century. He tri-
umphed over Heinrich von Ofterdingen in that poetic contest
at Wartburg Castle, known in literary history as the War of
Wartburg.

Page 67. *Like imperial Charlemagne.*

Charlemagne may be called by pre-eminence the monarch
of farmers. According to the German tradition, in seasons of
great abundance, his spirit crosses the Rhine on a golden
bridge at Bingen, and blesses the cornfields and the vineyards.
During his lifetime, he did not disdain, says Montesquieu,
"to sell the eggs from the farm-yards of his domains, and the
superfluous vegetables of his gardens; while he distributed
among his people the wealth of the Lombards and the im-
mense treasures of the Huns."

Page 203. *Behold, at last,*
Each tall and tapering mast
Is swung into its place.

I wish to anticipate a criticism on this passage by stating, that sometimes, though not usually, vessels are launched fully sparred and rigged. I have availed myself of the exception as better suited to my purposes than the general rule ; but the reader will see that it is neither a blunder nor a poetic license. On this subject a friend in Portland, Maine, writes me thus : —

"In this State, and also, I am told, in New York, ships are sometimes rigged upon the stocks, in order to save time, or to make a show. There was a fine, large ship launched last summer at Ellsworth, fully sparred and rigged. Some years ago a ship was launched here, with her rigging, spars, sails, and cargo aboard. She sailed the next day and — was never heard of again ! I hope this will not be the fate of your poem!"

Page 214. *Sir Humphrey Gilbert.*

" When the wind abated and the vessels were near enough, the Admiral was seen constantly sitting in the stern, with a book in his hand. On the 9th of September he was seen for the last time, and was heard by the people of the Hind to say, ' We are as near heaven by sea as by land.' In the following night, the lights of the ship suddenly disappeared. The people in the other vessel kept a good lookout for him during the remainder of the voyage. On the 22d of September they arrived, through much tempest and peril, at Falmouth. But nothing more was seen or heard of the Admiral." — BEL-KNAP's *American Biography*, I. 203.

Page 245. *The Blind Girl of Castèl-Cuillè.*

Jasmin, the author of this beautiful poem, is to the South of France what Burns is to the South of Scotland, — the representative of the heart of the people, — one of those happy bards who are born with their mouths full of birds (*la bouco pleno d'aouzelous*). He has written his own biography in a poetic form, and the simple narrative of his poverty, his struggles, and his triumphs, is very touching. He still lives at Agen, on the Garonne; and long may he live there to delight his native land with native songs!

The following description of his person and way of life is taken from the graphic pages of "Béarn and the Pyrenees," by Louisa Stuart Costello, whose charming pen has done so much to illustrate the French provinces and their literature.

"At the entrance of the promenade, Du Gravier, is a row of small houses, — some *cafés*, others shops, the indication of which is a painted cloth placed across the way, with the owner's name in bright gold letters, in the manner of the arcades in the streets, and their announcements. One of the most glaring of these was, we observed, a bright blue flag, bordered with gold; on which, in large gold letters, appeared the name of 'Jasmin, Coiffeur.' We entered, and were welcomed by a smiling, dark-eyed woman, who informed us that her husband was busy at that moment dressing a customer's hair, but he was desirous to receive us, and begged we would walk into his parlor at the back of the shop.

"She exhibited to us a laurel crown of gold, of delicate workmanship, sent from the city of Clemence Isaure, Toulouse, to the poet; who will probably one day take his place in the *capitoul*. Next came a golden cup, with an inscription in his honor, given by the citizens of Auch; a gold watch, chain, and seals, sent by the king, Louis Philippe; an emerald ring worn and presented by the lamented Duke of Orleans; a pearl pin, by the graceful Duchess, who, on the poet's visit to Paris accompanied by his son, received him in the words he puts into the mouth of Henri Quatre: —

> 'Brabes Gascous!
> A moun amou per bous aou dibes creyre:
> Benès! benès! ey plazé de bous beyre:
> Aproucha bous!'

A fine service of linen, the offering of the town of Pau, after
its citizens had given fêtes in his honor, and loaded him with
caresses and praises; and knickknacks and jewels of all descrip-
tions offered to him by lady-ambassadresses, and great lords;
English 'misses' and 'miladis'; and French, and foreigners
of all nations who did or did not understand Gascon.

"All this, though startling, was not convincing; Jasmin,
the barber, might only be a fashion, a *furore*, a caprice, after
all; and it was evident that he knew how to get up a scene
well. When we had become nearly tired of looking over
these tributes to his genius, the door opened, and the poet
himself appeared. His manner was free and unembarrassed,
well-bred, and lively; he received our compliments naturally,
and like one accustomed to homage; said he was ill, and un-
fortunately too hoarse to read anything to us, or should have
been delighted to do so. He spoke with a broad Gascon ac-
cent, and very rapidly and eloquently; ran over the story of
his successes; told us that his grandfather had been a beggar,
and all his family very poor; that he was now as rich as he
wished to be; his son placed in a good position at Nantes;
then showed us his son's picture, and spoke of his disposition;
to which his brisk little wife added, that, though no fool, he
had not his father's genius, to which truth Jasmin assented as
a matter of course. I told him of having seen mention made
of him in an English review; which he said had been sent
him by Lord Durham, who had paid him a visit; and I then
spoke of 'Me cal mouri' as known to me. This was enough
to make him forget his hoarseness and every other evil: it
would never do for me to imagine that that little song was his
best composition; it was merely his first; he must try to read
to me a little of 'L'Abuglo,'—a few verses of 'Françouneto.' 'You will be charmed,' said he; 'but if I were well,
and you would give me the pleasure of your company for some
time, if you were not merely running through Agen, I would

kill you with weeping, — I would make you die with distress for my poor Margarido, — my pretty Françouneto ! '

· " He caught up two copies of his book, from a pile lying on the table, and making us sit close to him, he pointed out the French translation on one side, which he told us to follow while he read in Gascon. He began in a rich, soft voice, and as he advanced, the surprise of Hamlet on hearing the player-king recite the disasters of Hecuba was but a type of ours, to find ourselves carried away by the spell of his enthusiasm. His eyes swam in tears ; he became pale and red ; he trembled ; he recovered himself ; his face was now joyous, now exulting, gay, jocose ; in fact, he was twenty actors in one ; he rang the changes from Rachel to Bouffé ; and he finished by delighting us, besides beguiling us of our tears, and overwhelming us with astonishment.

" He would have been a treasure on the stage ; for he is still, though his first youth is past, remarkably good-looking and striking ; with black, sparkling eyes, of intense expression ; a fine, ruddy complexion ; a countenance of wondrous mobility ; a good figure ; and action full of fire and grace ; he has handsome hands, which he uses with infinite effect ; and, on the whole, he is the best actor of the kind I ever saw. I could now quite understand what a troubadour or *jongleur* might be, and I look upon Jasmin as a revived specimen of that extinct race. Such as he is might have been Gaucelm Faidit, of Avignon, the friend of Cœur de Lion, who lamented the death of the hero in such moving strains ; such might have been Bernard de Ventadour, who sang the praises of Queen Elinore's beauty ; such Geoffrey Rudel, of Blaye, on his own Garonne ; such the wild Vidal : certain it is, that none of these troubadours of old could more move, by their singing or reciting, than Jasmin, in whom all their long-smothered fire and traditional magic seems reillumined.

" We found we had stayed hours instead of minutes with

the poet ; but he would not hear of any apology, — only re-
gretted that his voice was so out of tune, in consequence of a
violent cold, under which he was really laboring, and hoped
to see us again.   He told us our countrywomen of Pau had
laden him with kindness and attention, and spoke with such
enthusiasm of the beauty of certain 'misses,' that I feared his
little wife would feel somewhat piqued ; but, on the contrary,
she stood by, smiling and happy, and enjoying the stories of
his triumphs.   I remarked that he had restored the poetry of
the troubadours ; asked him if he knew their songs ; and said
he was worthy to stand at their head.   ' I am, indeed, a troubadour,' said he, with energy ; ' but I am far beyond them all :
they were but beginners ; they never composed a poem like
my Françouneto ! there are no poets in France now, — there
cannot be ; the language does not admit of it ; where is the
fire, the spirit, the expression, the tenderness, the force of the
Gascon ?   French is but the ladder to reach to the first floor of
Gascon, — how can you get up to a height except by a ladder ! '

    .   .   .   .

"I returned by Agen, after an absence in the Pyrenees of
some months, and renewed my acquaintance with Jasmin and
his dark-eyed wife.   I did not expect that I should be recognized ; but the moment I entered the little shop I was hailed
as an old friend.   'Ah !' cried Jasmin, 'enfin la voilà
encore !'   I could not but be flattered by this recollection,
but soon found it was less on my own account that I was thus
welcomed, than because a circumstance had occurred to the
poet which he thought I could perhaps explain.   He produced
several French newspapers, in which he pointed out to me an
article headed 'Jasmin à Londres' ; being a translation of certain notices of himself, which had appeared in a leading English literary journal.   He had, he said, been informed of the
honor done him by numerous friends, and assured me his fame

had been much spread by this means ; and he was so delighted on the occasion, that he had resolved to learn English, in
order that he might judge of the translations from his works,
which, he had been told, were well done. I enjoyed his surprise, while I informed him that I knew who was the reviewer
and translator ; and explained the reason for the verses giving
pleasure in an English dress to be the superior simplicity of
the English language over Modern French, for which he has a
great contempt, as unfitted for lyrical composition. He in-
quired of me respecting Burns, to whom he had been likened ;
and begged me to tell him something of Moore. The delight
of himself and his wife was amusing, at having discovered a
secret which had puzzled them so long.

"He had a thousand things to tell me ; in particular, that
he had only the day before received a letter from the Duchess
of Orleans, informing him that she had ordered a medal of her
late husband to be struck, the first of which would be sent to
him : she also announced to him the agreeable news of the
king having granted him a pension of a thousand francs. He
smiled and wept by turns, as he told us all this ; and declared,
much as he was elated at the possession of a sum which made
him a rich man for life, the kindness of the Duchess gratified
him even more.

"He then made us sit down while he read us two new poems ; both charming, and full of grace and *naïveté;* and one
very affecting, being an address to the king, alluding to the
death of his son. As he read, his wife stood by, and fearing
we did not quite comprehend his language, she made a remark
to that effect : to which he answered impatiently, 'Nonsense,
— don't you see they are in tears.' This was unanswerable ;
and we were allowed to hear the poem to the end ; and I cer-
tainly never listened to anything more feelingly and energeti-
cally delivered.

"We had much conversation, for he was anxious to detain

us, and, in the course of it, he told me he had been by some accused of vanity. 'O,' he rejoined, what would you have! I am a child of nature, and cannot conceal my feelings; the only difference between me and a man of refinement is, that he knows how to conceal his vanity and exultation at success, which I let everybody see.'"—*Béarn and the Pyrenees*, I. 369, *et seq.*

Page 262. *A Christmas Carol.*

The following description of Christmas in Burgundy is from M. Fertiault's *Coup d'Œil sur les Noels en Bourgogne*, prefixed to the Paris edition of *Les Noels Bourguignons de Bernard de la Monnoye* (*Gui Barôzai*), 1842.

"Every year at the approach of Advent, people refresh their memories, clear their throats, and begin preluding, in the long evenings by the fireside, those carols whose invariable and eternal theme is the coming of the Messiah. They take from old closets pamphlets, little collections begrimed with dust and smoke, to which the press, and sometimes the pen, has consigned these songs; and as soon as the first Sunday of Advent sounds, they gossip, they gad about, they sit together by the fireside, sometimes at one house, sometimes at another, taking turns in paying for the chestnuts and white wine, but singing with one common voice the grotesque praises of the *Little Jesus*. There are very few villages even, which, during all the evenings of Advent, do not hear some of these curious canticles shouted in their streets, to the nasal drone of bagpipes. In this case the minstrel comes as a reinforcement to the singers at the fireside; he brings and adds his dose of joy (spontaneous or mercenary, it matters little which) to the joy which breathes around the hearth-stone; and when the voices vibrate and resound, one voice more is always welcome. There, it is not the purity of the notes which makes the concert, but the quantity, — *non qualitas, sed quantitas;* then, (to finish at once with the minstrel,) when the Saviour has at length been born in the manger, and the beautiful Christmas Eve is passed, the rustic piper makes his round among the houses, where every one compliments and thanks him, and, moreover, gives him in small coin the price of the shrill notes with which he has enlivened the evening entertainments.

"More or less until Christmas Eve, all goes on in this way among our devout singers, with the difference of some gallons of wine or some hundreds of chestnuts. But this famous eve once come, the scale is pitched upon a higher key; the closing evening must be a memorable one. The toilet is begun at nightfall; then comes the hour of supper, admonishing divers appetites; and groups, as numerous as possible, are formed to take together this comfortable evening repast. The supper finished, a circle gathers around the hearth, which is arranged and set in order this evening after a particular fashion, and which at a later hour of the night is to become the object of special interest to the children. On the burning brands an enormous log has been placed. This log assuredly does not change its nature, but it changes its name during this evening: it is called the *Suche* (the Yule-log). 'Look you,' say they to the children, 'if you are good this evening, Noel' (for with children one must always personify) 'will rain down sugar-plums in the night.' And the children sit demurely, keeping as quiet as their turbulent little natures will permit. The groups of older persons, not always as orderly as the children, seize this good opportunity to surrender themselves with merry hearts and boisterous voices to the chanted worship of the miraculous Noel. For this final solemnity, they have kept the most powerful, the most enthusiastic, the most electrifying carols. Noel! Noel! Noel! This magic word resounds on all sides; it seasons every sauce, it is served up with every course. Of the thousands of canticles which are heard on this famous eve, ninety-nine in a hundred begin and end with this word; which is, one may say, their Alpha and Omega, their crown and footstool. This last evening, the merry-making is prolonged. Instead of retiring at ten or eleven o'clock, as is generally done on all the preceding evenings, they wait for the stroke of midnight: this word sufficiently proclaims to what ceremony they are going to repair. For ten minutes or a quarter of an hour, the bells have been calling the faithful with a triple-bob-major; and each one, furnished with a little taper streaked with various colors, (the Christmas Candle,) goes through the crowded streets, where the lanterns are dancing like Will-o'-the-Wisps, at the impatient summons of the multitudinous chimes. It is the Midnight Mass. Once inside the church, they hear with more or less piety the Mass, emblematic of the coming of the Messiah. Then in tumult and great haste they return homeward, always in numerous groups; they salute the Yule-log; they pay homage to the hearth; they sit down at table; and, amid songs which reverberate louder than ever, make this meal of after-Christmas, so long looked for, so cherished, so joyous, so noisy, and which it has been thought fit to call, we hardly know why, *Rossignon.* The supper eaten at nightfall is no impediment, as you may imagine, to the appetite's returning; above all, if the going to and from church has made the devout eaters feel some little shafts of the sharp and biting north-wind. *Rossignon* then goes on merrily, — sometimes far into the morning hours; but, nevertheless, gradually throats grow hoarse, stomachs are filled, the Yule-log burns out, and at last the hour arrives when each one, as best he may, regains his domicile and his bed, and puts with himself between the sheets the material for a good sore-throat, or a good indigestion, for the morrow. Previous to this, care has been taken to place in the slippers, or wooden shoes of the children, the sugar-plums, which shall be for them, on their waking, the welcome fruits of the Christmas log."

In the Glossary, the *Suche*, or Yule-log, is thus defined : —

"This is a huge log, which is placed on the fire on Christmas Eve, and which in Burgundy is called, on this account, *lai Suche de Noei*. Then the father of the family, particularly among the middle classes, sings solemnly Christmas carols with his wife and children, the smallest of whom he sends into the corner to pray that the Yule-log may bear him some sugar-plums. Meanwhile, little parcels of them are placed under each end of the log, and the children come and pick them up, believing, in good faith, that the great log has borne them."

Cambridge : Printed by Welch, Bigelow, & Co.

CPSIA information can be obtained
at www.ICGtesting.com
Printed in the USA
BVOW09*1616021117
499244BV00008B/121/P